DISCARDED

MORRIS
MINOR

Also by this author:

GREAT CARS OF THE WORLD

MORRIS
MINOR
Exploring the legend

Jon Pressnell

First published in June 1998

British Library Cataloguing in Publication Data:
A catalogue record for this book is available from the British Library

ISBN 1 85960 429 3

Library of Congress catalog card no. 98-70519

Haynes Publishing, Sparkford,
Nr Yeovil, Somerset, BA22 7JJ.
Tel: 01963 440635 Fax: 01963 440001
Int. tel: +44 1963 440635
Int fax: +44 1963 440001

E-mail: sales@haynes-manuals.co.uk
Web site: http://www.haynes.com

Haynes North America, Inc.
861 Lawrence Drive, Newbury Park,
California 91320 USA

Designed & typeset by
G&M, Raunds, Northamptonshire

Printed in Great Britain by
J. H. Haynes & Co. Ltd

Contents

Introduction

THIS BOOK IS not a history of the Morris Minor. Rather, it is an exploration of different aspects of the Minor, many of which have hitherto not been studied in any depth.

Drawing on the memories of those who were there, and on surviving Morris Motors archive material, the historical chapters answer, I hope, many of the questions up until now unanswered. What you'll read here is in many instances being revealed for the first time.

The book also looks in detail at the Minor's little-known Australian big brother, the Major, and examines such topics as the Alta conversion, the Minor in the States, and how to put a Fiat twin-cam engine into your Morris.

If that seems a bit too much like hard work, you'll also find illustrated in full colour every Minor sales catalogue you're likely to come across, and a chapter devoted to Morris Minor models.

Finally, for all those of you who wish you could still buy a new Minor – in one form or another – four of Britain's top stylists present their ideas on a 'Minor for the Millennium'. They explain their thoughts in detail, and their exclusive artwork should certainly start a few lively arguments.

In the Morris's 50th birthday year, this book is both a tribute to the Minor and a testimony to the car's enduring appeal and versatility. Here's to the next half century!

Jon Pressnell, 1998

Acknowledgements

THIS BOOK WOULD not have been possible without the help of so many people who gave generously of their time. Jack Daniels in particular has made a major contribution, through two long interviews, and was also kind enough to read and comment upon some of the manuscript.

Other former Nuffield/BMC engineers to whom thanks are due are Fred Coultas, Charles Griffin, John Sheppard, Gerald Palmer, Chris Kingham, Rod Bull, Jim Lambert, and the late Reg Job. On the flat-four engine, former Morris Engines Branch employees Tony Jennings, Mark Yeatman-Reed, Eric Hill, John Barker, Harry Gray and Fred Collis have provided valued insights; I am grateful to Stuart Smith of the *Coventry Evening Telegraph* for helping me make contact.

Thanks also go to Dr Alex Moulton, for information on suspension systems, and to John Hopkins for his help in analysing the flat-four engine.

For the chapter on the Wolseley Eight engine, Series E owner Martin Wills and Wolseley Eight owner Dave Bates kindly let me drive their cars; thanks are also due to Dave Allen and Tony Hawksworth of the Wolseley Register. The chapter on the Alta conversion owes much to Graham Holt and to Sandy and Rosie Hamilton, with further assistance from Stuart Derrington, Mollie Cain, Ian Dussek and Ted Napper.

The models chapter features the collections of Bryan Gostling and Richard Cownden, and the sales catalogues reproduced between chapters are also from the Cownden and Gostling collections; many thanks go to both these long-time MMOC members, and also to Dave and Lesley Price for their further help with the models chapter.

Over in America, Tony Burgess, Jon Merker and Tony Martinis greatly assisted, as did Paul Blank, Judy Ayrton and Don Slater in Australia, and Anton Kamp Nielsen (of Nordisk Morris Minor Lager) in Denmark.

For their superb renderings of a Minor for the '90s I am extremely grateful to Peter Horbury, Ian Callum, Peter Stevens and James Watkins for fitting the project into their hectic schedules; thanks also go to Kevin Jones and Geoff Upex of Rover, and to the press offices of Rover, Renault, Citroën, Mazda and Volkswagen.

John and Robin Beardmore updated me on their meticulous Fiat twin-cam conversions, and further information came from Nick Spanakis of Minor Mania and Stuart Holmes of Mighty Minors. Others who have helped in various ways are Lucy Brown, David Knowles, and Andrew Booth and Liz Saxon of the Morris Minor Owners' Club.

The minutes of Morris and Nuffield board meetings are quoted with acknowledgement to the British Motor Industry Heritage Trust and with thanks to guardians the Modern Record

Centre, University of Warwick; quotations from the Miles Thomas papers are by courtesy of BMIHT. As ever, my sincerest thanks go to Anders Clausager, Karam Ram and Richard Brotherton at the Heritage Motor Centre, for their many kindnesses in the course of research for this book, and for the provision of so many of the archive photos used.

The chapters on Jack Daniels, on the Minors that never were, on the Morris Major, and on Fiat twin-cam conversions are expanded and updated versions of articles that first appeared in *Classic and Sports Car* magazine, and are used with acknowledgement and with thanks to the editor. The colour photos of the brochures and models are the work of James Mann.

Chapter One

Sir Alec Issigonis 1906–1988

THE MINOR WAS largely the creation of one man, in a way that would be impossible to imagine in today's motor industry. That man was Sir Alec Issigonis CBE FRS, one of the greatest and most inspired motor engineers of the 20th century.

Issigonis brought to car design a single-mindedness and an intuitive originality that have never been equalled. Sometimes the results bordered on the idiosyncratic, but an Issigonis design was invariably founded on sound – and often subtle – engineering principles. And always his aims were the same: excellent road manners, space efficiency, compactness, and – at least to some degree – the subservience of style to function.

Born in 1906, in Smyrna, Turkey, Issigonis had his big break when he joined Morris Motors in 1936, to work on independent front suspension systems, then a major preoccupation within the motor industry. Before this he had spent the period 1928–34 working with the inventor Edward Gillett to perfect Gillett's automatic clutch mechanism; this had been followed by a spell with Rootes, where he worked on the Humber/Hillman 'Evenkeel' independent front suspension.

The coil-and-wishbone front end Issigonis designed for Morris, complete with then advanced rack-and-pinion steering, was intended for the Series M Morris Ten; it ultimately emerged on the post-war $1^{1}/_{4}$-litre MG saloon, and could still be seen, in modified form, on the final MGB of 1980.

During this pre-war period Issigonis, with his friend George Dowson, spent much spare-time effort designing and building a characteristically innovative

Broad felt-tip uncapped, Alec Issigonis makes a point. On the desk are the inevitable sketches. (Haymarket)

hillclimb Austin Seven single-seater, the famous Lightweight Special. Although home-constructed, without the use of power tools, the elegant little machine was more advanced than most Grand Prix cars of the day. In particular it had a brilliantly conceived monocoque form of construction in which many elements were given a structural function with which they would not normally have been entrusted; it also had rubber springing, with rubber discs at the front and rubber loops in tension at the rear. The Lightweight Special was an invaluable test-bed for Issigonis's ideas: the lessons that would ultimately lead to the Mini were in the process of being learned.

By this time Project Engineer for all Morris cars, Issigonis was kept occupied for much of the war by various military projects, including armoured cars and an amphibious tank. All the same, by the end of 1943 he and his draughtsmen Jack Daniels and Reg Job had designed and built a little two-seat runabout that united in one vehicle all his most advanced thinking on passenger cars. This was the car soon known as the 'Mosquito', and from it sprang – as is related elsewhere – the Morris Minor.

The Mosquito was very much Issigonis's own personal vision of how a small car should be, even if it seemingly picked up much of its inspiration from sources as diverse as Citroën, Steyr and – stylistically, at least – the American Packard.

It was a car of many subtle details, but more particularly it was one of the industry's first fully integrated designs. Thus the front suspension with its long centrally anchored torsion bars and bulkhead-mounted upper links not only made for a supple ride but also spread structural stresses, while the unusually small 14-inch wheels gave increased

The Lightweight Special was an exquisitely formed and brilliantly engineered racer, built with hand tools by Issigonis and George Dowson. Taken at Silverstone in 1960, this photo shows Issigonis at the wheel, and Dowson (in tie) helping push-start the car. (Motor Sport/LAT)

No photos of the Alvis V8 are known, but this specially commissioned artwork gives an accurate impression of how it would have looked. (Brian Hatton/Classic & Sports Car)

passenger space as well as reducing unsprung weight and harmonising with the car's overall proportions. Most notably, a key element of the original design was a flat-four engine, as fully discussed in Chapter Three. The result, when launched in 1948 as the Minor, was a car with a wheel-at-each-corner stance, excellent space utilisation, and first-class roadholding and handling — characteristics that would be seen in all Issigonis's subsequent designs, but most particularly in the Mini.

Inspired by the Citroën *Traction Avant*, Issigonis would have liked the Minor to have had front-wheel drive — 'but I did not know how to do it at the time,' he later admitted. By 1952, though, he felt sufficiently confident to be able to initiate the construction of a transverse-engined fwd Minor. He was not around, however, to see the car's satisfactory completion, as Alvis had lured him to Coventry, with a free

hand to design an all-new sports saloon.

Compact, very light, and packed with ingenious features, the Issigonis car was powered by a $3^1/2$-litre alloy V8, and used a two-speed gearbox in unit with the differential, with overdrive on both gears — typical 'Issi' originality intended to give the Alvis a degree of automaticity. The car cemented Issigonis's personal and professional friendship with suspension engineer Alex Moulton, a collaboration that had begun with an experimental rubber-sprung Minor. Moulton initially equipped the Alvis with a form of rubber springing and latterly with a rubber/fluid system; ultimately inter-connected front to rear, this was a pro-totype of the Hydrolastic system used in the future on the 1100 and on other BMC cars.

Alas, Alvis found that it could not justify expenditure on a new car, and cancelled the whole project. At the end of 1955 BMC chief Leonard Lord asked

Issigonis back, to be Chief Engineer at BMC, with a free hand to develop new cars for the organisation.

On his return to BMC Issigonis led what would today be called a 'think tank' – a small group exploring future product concepts. The first prototype to emerge was a rear-wheel-drive 1$\frac{1}{2}$-litre saloon coded XC9001. Equipped with a development of the Alvis V8's Moulton fluid-and-rubber suspension, it had simple four-light styling that presaged that of the Mini.

After this came a smaller car with similar looks, intended to be a replacement for the Minor. Called XC9002, this was the starting-point for what became the 1100. But before Issigonis could get stuck in, the Suez crisis forced a postponement: Leonard Lord wanted the team instead to produce a small saloon to sweep the then voguish bubble-cars off the British roads. This, of course, became the Mini. Ironically, given its cult status and its extraordinarily long life, the Mini was the last production car to be wholly designed by Issigonis. Although emphatically his concepts, both the 1100 and the 1800 were entrusted for their development to others, as were the Austin 3-litre and the Maxi.

Both the major designs, the 1100 and the 1800, were logical extensions of the Issigonis philosophy, and he was particularly proud of the 1800, which had a remarkable spaciousness and many clever details in the arrangement of its suspension and in its overall structure.

While these projects were making their way towards production, Issigonis was also directing work on a family of V4 and V6 engines, which he saw as the ideal solution to his quest for compact power units for front-wheel-drive installation. Both the 1800 and the MGB were initially schemed around the V4, but the V-engine programme was cancelled by a cash-strapped BMC.

As Engineering Director of BMC from 1964, Issigonis had a continuing involvement in future product planning, and one of the more surprising cars for which he had responsibility was a Hydrolastic-sprung sports car powered by the 4-litre Rolls-Royce engine used in the Vanden Plas 4-litre R; this stillborn white elephant was intended as a rival to the Jaguar E-type, and was notable for its exceptional torsional rigidity.

But small cars were Issigonis's real love, and in 1966 or thereabouts he asked to be relieved of all other projects

XC9002 (foreground) and XC9001, photographed in the Experimental Department at Longbridge. The smaller XC9002 started out as a replacement for the Minor, and evolved into the 1100; XC9001 remained a one-off 'ideas car'. (BMIHT/Rover)

so that he could concentrate on the creation of a replacement for the Mini. While he had an enduring fondness for the Mini, an engineer such as Issigonis never stood still, and he was convinced that with a clean sheet of paper he could evolve a new world-beater.

The resultant car, tagged '9X', proved the point – and showed that Issigonis had lost none of his old magic. Even shorter than the Mini, the crisp little hatchback was more spacious, was to have been significantly cheaper to make, and in its ultimate form could have been powered by a six-cylinder 1.3-litre engine. With its ingeniously compact engine and gearbox, '9X' was arguably Issigonis's greatest achievement after the Mini itself. Alas, the frail health of BMC led to the merger with Leyland, and a combination of internal politics and the pressing need to produce a new mid-range car put paid to this exciting project. Issigonis continued with the car's development, however, and indeed in his retirement ran around Birmingham in a superficially standard Mini that in fact used '9X' mechanicals.

Sidelined by BL's ex-Triumph managers, Issigonis turned his attention to experimentation with steam propulsion and hydrostatic transmission. He retired from the company at the end of 1971, but was retained as a consultant, with a design office at Longbridge. He carried on working even when ill-health kept him housebound, receiving daily visits from the company engineer who had been detailed to him.

In these last years his chief activities were developing an ingenious gearless transmission, and investigating refinements to the Mini.

Sir Alec Issigonis – he was knighted in 1969 – died in October 1988. To the end his mind was as sharp as ever, and to the end he carried on working. As a colleague of his remarked, 'he lived and slept motor cars'.

It's often said, with justice, that Issigonis's cars very much reflected his personality. So just what sort of a person was he?

'To be with him was absolutely inspirational,' remembers John Sheppard, who worked on body engineering with Issigonis. 'Everything he thought of was a challenge.'

Fred Coultas, a former Rover Group senior engineer now running BMIHT, has equally strong memories of his one-time chief. 'You couldn't help but be in awe of him, because ideas would just flow from his brain so fast . . . He knew where he wanted to go, he knew what he wanted, and that took months and months out of a programme, because there was no debate. He was a very impatient guy, though, because his mind was racing on so far ahead. Once I was doing some cooling system tests for him, and they took quite a time – 2 or 3 hours. But Sir Alec would have

none of that. "Come on," he'd say. "I want the answer, I want the answer *now*!" . . .'

Rod Bull, the Austin Rover engineer detailed to Issigonis in his last years, remembers Sir Alec for his 'superb engineering common sense', for his 'incredibly dry sense of humour' – and for his sharpness of mind. 'With Sir Alec it was a bit like Occam's Razor – when you cut through all the chaff and the kernel pops up immediately. He was very good at getting straight to the heart of a question.

'Very often I'd set out to present all the data to him, for him to make the decision. He'd just ask, "Does it or doesn't it work?" And I'd say, "Well, it's got its good points and its bad points." Then he'd say, in a slightly harsher tone, "*Does* it or *doesn't* it work?"'

John Sheppard recalls another famous trait: 'His ability to sketch was absolutely fantastic. I've never come across anyone quite like him.'

This attribute – he'd sketch on everything from a concrete floor to a table-cloth – is also remembered by Charles Griffin, former BMC Chief Engineer and the man responsible for developing the 1100.

'His major strength was this ability he had to produce a rapid design. He was able to create something literally as he was ploughing along with his pencil. That made him pretty unique.

'In this he was a natural. He hadn't got too much time for the mathematics, for the calculations. But he had that amazing eye, and he recognised that engineering obeyed natural laws. He was able to visualise things and put them down on paper in proportion, so that if a stress engineer picked up something he'd done, he'd find it uniformly correct, within small margins. In that respect he was pretty unique . . . As an all-round engineer, I should think he's unbeaten.'

Totally devoted to his craft as he was, Issigonis was no modest recluse, beavering away silently at his drawing-board or busying himself with the model aeroplanes and steam engines he so loved. His clarity of vision was matched by a self-belief that was sometimes hidden by a certain diffidence, but was equally often rather more outgoing – hence the soubriquet 'Arrogonis' about which he was known to jest.

'I used to call him the Noel Coward of the motor industry,' says former colleague Gerald Palmer. 'When Coward put on a play, *he* wrote it, *he* choreographed it. Issigonis was a bit like that. Someone once called him a ballerina . . .'

Charles Griffin confirms this view of Issigonis as showman. 'He was very sociable, so long as he was the centre of the happening. He had to be the focal point, otherwise he got bored.

'He didn't fit the normal mould for an engineer. There was nobody like him, except his old pal John Morris, the chief engineer at SU Carburetters. They were like they'd stepped right out of the pages of Dickens – they argued about nothing at all, so long as it had a technical connection. They once had a big argument about the potential power output of a human being. John Morris swore that a man was capable of transmitting 1 horsepower for I think 10 seconds. And he proceeded to prove it, with a stopwatch in his hand, dashing

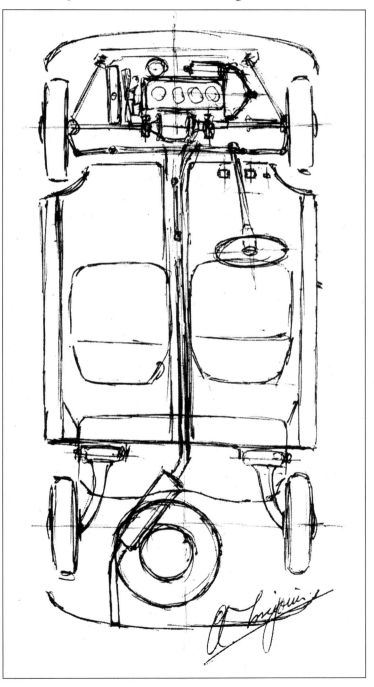

This typical quickfire yet accurate sketch by Issigonis shows the basic Mini layout, at a stage before subframes were introduced. (Author's collection)

up and down the stairs, having weighed himself. He collapsed with a heart attack before he was able to confirm or deny it . . .'

Such a man as Issigonis could never create a dull car. Quirky and flawed though many of his designs are, they are all essentially honest cars, with a style born out of a refreshing devotion to function and to engineering first principles. Issigonis brought charm, style and engineering flair to the popular car, yet with an uncompromised purity of intention and execution. The Minor, as the Mini that followed, is an intensely personal car, bearing the unmistakable Issigonis stamp, and like the Mini it stands as a lasting monument to a landmark figure in the history of the motor car.

Chapter Two

Jack Daniels and the Minor

'I GOT ON with him excellently. We just gelled together, as simple as that. He knew what he wanted, and was prepared to allow me to do it . . .'

For more than 30 years, engineer Jack Daniels worked closely with Sir Alec Issigonis, interpreting and developing his ideas and refining them for production. On his retirement in 1977, Daniels was Chief Engineer, Advanced Vehicles, for BL Cars, but at the time of the Minor he was Chief Design and Development Engineer at the Nuffield Organisation's Cowley base.

Along with body draughtsman Reg Job he was thus one of the team of three – Issigonis, Daniels and Job – that shaped the Morris Minor from its earliest days as the narrow-bodied Morris Mosquito through to such later developments as the front-wheel-drive Minor of circa 1952; his responsibility was the running gear.

Daniels began his career in 1927, as an apprentice at MG's Edmund Road plant in Cowley, moving to MG's new home in Abingdon around three years later as a draughtsman. At Abingdon he worked with MG's famed Chief Designer, H. N. Charles, on the R-Type Midget single-seater, with its advanced but not totally satisfactory all-independent suspension, and on a prototype six-cylinder saloon using similar all-round independent suspension by torsion bars. This was the car coded EX150, and nicknamed the 'Queen Mary'; it was to have had a $3^1/_2$-litre

engine, quite likely a derivative of the 25hp Wolseley Super Six unit.

When the MG design office at Abingdon was closed down in 1935 and MG design transferred to the

Daniels in 1988, photographed with the author's Minor. (Matt Barnes/Classic & Sports Car)

Morris works at Cowley, Daniels moved over as well, still as a draughtsman on MG projects. In 1936/37 he was transferred to the office of Alec Issigonis – then freshly recruited from Rootes, and working on front suspension systems.

Daniels worked with Issigonis on a coil-and-wishbone suspension in conjunction with the then advanced feature of rack-and-pinion steering, the whole package being intended for what would, at its October 1938 launch, become the Morris Ten Series 'M'. In the end, however, the 'M' was given a cheaper beam axle, this being a particularly subtle design by H. N. Charles. The

Issigonis assembly was instead slated for introduction on a small MG saloon tentatively called the MG Ten. This emerged after the war, as the 1¼-litre MG YA, and its Issigonis front suspension was still to be seen in its essentials on the last MGB of 1980.

During much of the war Daniels worked away from Issigonis, and was responsible, among other things, for a monocoque reconnaissance car and an 85-ton tank. Both have relevance to the Minor: the reconnaissance car used a bent torsion bar for the front springing, while the tank used no fewer than 32 torsion bars, 8 feet long and $2^3/_8$ inches in diameter, and led to the construction of a special rig for the testing of torsion bars.

Creating the Mosquito

It is thought that the conception of the Minor dates to 1941. Certainly by 1942 a scale model had been built, looking uncannily like the final article. By March 1943 the prototype bare shell had been built, and by the end of the year this first 'ideas car' had been completed, and was tagged the Mosquito. In its styling it was well in advance of pre-war British offerings, and reflected American trends of the time.

'Issigonis had quite a liking for some of the American cars – apart from the garish ones, which he didn't like at all,' remembers Daniels. 'The more simply styled ones, such as the Chevrolet, he really had a fancy for – oh yes. I can still see an American flavour to the Minor.'

Suspension design

Torsion bar suspension was always part of the new car's concept. At least in part this was a result of the inspirational example of the *Traction Avant* Citroën, which used torsion bars front and rear. 'We were all very impressed by it,' says Daniels. 'At Citroën they had the

most advanced suspension people in the world.

'Torsion bars were damned expensive things at the time, but we sat down and learned how to make them less expensively, working with a chap called Frank Ford at Wolseley.

'We knew we couldn't afford torsion bar failure, so we set ourselves a target of 100,000 stress cycles. Using our special rig, we found ourselves just missing this 100,000 cycles – we were averaging around 95,000 cycles . . . . We sat down and said, "What can we do?", and ended up choosing shot-peening. After this, we were talking half a million cycles. We had to take the bars off the rig, because we hadn't the time.

'Despite this, the first ten months of Minors went through before the shot-peening was in use, but very obviously we had over-engineered: before I left for Longbridge in 1956 I had a check made through Service, to find out how many failed early torsion bars they'd had – and they showed me five.

'Two of them had had battery acid spilt on them, one of them had been in an accident, and two of them we could find nothing wrong with, so we put them back on the rig, and they did almost 100,000 cycles again . . .'

The actual suspension configuration for the front end was carefully thought out to minimise stresses both on the torsion bars and on the bodyshell, hence the length of the torsion bars and the height of the kingpins, so their upper arm could pick up on the bulkhead and thus spread the load more

Further sketches – taken, as with the earlier ones, from the BMC press-release booklet celebrating the millionth Minor. Issigonis obviously likes the vertical motif, as the grille treatment shown here is echoed in his treatment of the Mosquito's dashboard. (Issigonis/BMC)

The front suspension of the Minor is clearly shown in this BMC drawing. The longitudinal torsion bar is anchored at the central crossmember and the two-piece lower arm is located by a diagonal arm mounted in a rubber bush. The tall swivel pin with its threaded trunnions allows the upper arm, constituted by the lever-arm damper, to be mounted high on the bulkhead. (BMC)

surely. In addition, the suspension was designed to limit roll.

'Most people with independent front suspension – generally coils – were using anti-roll bars. We said, "We're not going to use anti-roll bars: we'll make our suspension just stiff enough that we don't need them, to save the cost of an anti-roll bar." By this time we knew where we'd gone wrong with the MG R-Type – we'd used equal-length wishbones all round . . .'

Thoughts on rear suspension

Torsion bar springing was originally schemed for the rear, with axle location aided by the use of a torque tube.

'We did have a go at a bent torsion bar on the rear of the Mosquito, coming from the back of the car to be secured at the central crossmember where the front torsion bars were anchored. It was used with a live back axle anchored by radius arms. It had characteristics we didn't like – odd steering troubles. We didn't try all that hard with it – we went instead for what was economic, and for what we had knowledge of, and sat down and really made the leaf-spring work. However, we left the crossmember exactly where it was in the first place, roughly central in the car.'

Such were his recollections when the author first interviewed Daniels in 1988. Today, on reflection, he feels that the car never in fact ran with a rear suspension using a bent torsion bar.

'We certainly got as far as drawing up this sort of arrangement. What put us off the idea, however, was not the torsion bar itself but the radius arms to which the axle was connected. What worried us was that as the axle started to move up and down we thought that under the stresses generated something had to give. Either the axle was going to give, or the radius arms, or a combination of both. So I don't remember us actually making up a rear axle like this, or us even taking it as far as testing the set-up on a rig. It would certainly have been drawn up, but in the end we funked it'.

However far down the line the experiments went, by April 1945 Morris memos confirm that a torsion-bar rear had been abandoned. But didn't the use of old-fashioned cart springs go against the grain for such an advanced thinker as Issigonis?

'No, it wasn't at all against the grain. We were quite happy using leaf-springs, but took what for that size of car was quite a long spring, to help us get neutral steering characteristics.'

That said, Issigonis did contemplate an independently suspended rear for the Minor, using swing axles neatly restrained by bent torsion bars; Daniels cannot recall the idea ever passing beyond the sketch stage.

The rejection of such radical thinking in favour of tried-and-tested solutions was probably in part a result of the influence of Nuffield's Chief Engineer, A. V. Oak.

'He kept a watching brief. I would say that Vic Oak was the man who in the main kept the most controversial – the most uneconomic – aspects of Issigonis's thoughts out of the car. He kept our feet on the ground. He was a very practical man, and he knew what you could make, and how you could make it. He kept us down on earth without imposing his will on the basic design at all.'

The engine question

The entire 'package' for the Minor was to be new, and an essential part of the whole was an Issigonis-designed flat-four engine, with side valves. The idea behind such an engine was to liberate more space for the passenger compartment, and to lower the car's centre of gravity.

The car was designed around this power unit, as testified by the wide engine bay; two versions were to be available – 800cc and 1100cc. Following American usage, a column gearchange was fitted to the first Mosquitoes, in conjunction with a bench front seat.

'Although 4 inches narrower than the production Minor, I drove the prototype with three people up front,' recalls Daniels. 'And the column change was beautiful, at a time when many column changes were very troublesome.'

As for the flat-four engine, the 1100cc version wasn't at all bad, he maintains.

'But the engine gave a side-valve performance. Side valves were used to avoid having to lengthen the whole engine sideways with an ohv pushrod mechanism – simple as that! The engine had to drop between the wheel arches

This left-hand-drive prototype is almost certainly EX/SX/131, and has the steering-column gearchange recalled by Daniels as being so sweet in its action. The octagonal surrounds to the speedo and clock are likely to have been additions during the period in 1947 when launching the Mosquito as an MG was being discussed. (BMIHT/Rover)

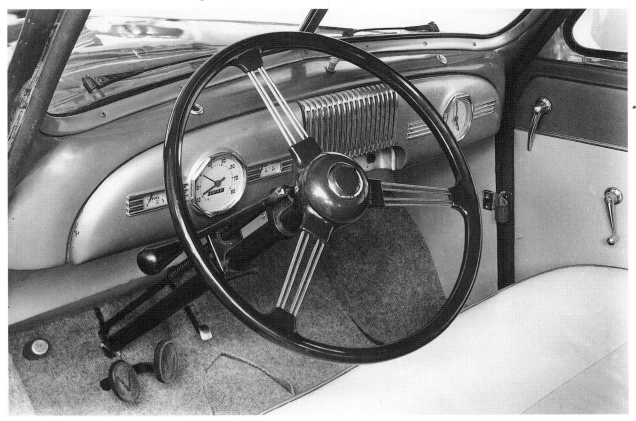

on a vehicle 4 inches narrower than you know it today, don't forget.'

But why didn't the Minor get its flat-four engine, ending up instead with the old side-valve 918cc in-line unit of the Morris Eight?

'The engine had to be built by our engine people in Coventry. Tom Brown was the man there, and he didn't want a flat-four engine, as he was designing his own range of overhead-cam engines. I'm convinced Morris Engines at Coventry did something that killed off our engine entirely.

'When we had run the engines they'd built for us, we had a problem with vibration. Quite a lot of time went by before we found the cause. What we'd

---

The Minor tougher than a Cadillac?

Yes it's true. Issigonis was very keen on testing as many vehicles as possible for their torsional stiffness, says Jack Daniels. The Minor was put in a rig and gave respectable figures of around 4,000lb ft needed for one degree of deflection. 'The A30/A35 had an exceptionally tough body – much too tough – and was up at about 9,000lb ft per degree,' recalls Daniels. 'But a Cadillac we tested could only manage something in the order of 1,000lb ft per degree'.

---

done originally was to take the flywheel and mount it straight on to the end of the crankshaft with four bolts passing through four dowel tubes.

'But when the engines came back from Coventry, what they'd done was to put dowel bolts in, instead of using dowel tubes through which bolts should have passed. The dowel part of the bolts they put in had to be a slack fit so that the bolts could align with the holes in the crank . . . and that gave us a vibration at the flywheel. Once we'd found out what it was, we simply inserted two dowels, and killed the problem stone-dead. But I'm afraid it was too late.

'I think it would have been too late anyway, because Lord Nuffield didn't like the engine. He was dead agin it –

he liked his own engines, not least the side-valve engine in the Morris Eight.

'As the flat-four ran into doubts, we would have liked to turn to the 918cc overhead-valve variant of the Eight engine, as used in the Wolseley Eight. But Lord Nuffield wanted a side-valve engine.

'Once it had been cancelled, that was it for the flat-four. The vibration had been a problem, and we didn't get the answer in time. Had we done so, it might have been more difficult to cancel it.'

The last prototype with the flat-four has a build date of April 1947, around which time Nuffield's senior management was in agonies of indecision over the Minor project — not helped by Lord Nuffield's oft-expressed opinion that there was little point in launching a radical new small car when Morris was selling as many of the existing Eight Series E as it could make.

Launch dates were constantly changed, revised Series E models proposed instead — including one with Minor front suspension and steering gear — and there was even talk of selling the car not as a Morris but as a high-spec MG. In this form it would have had an 1100cc ohc unit from Tom Brown's new family of engines. After this idea was abandoned and the Morris version revived, a side-valve adaptation of the ohc engine was considered, then a bored-out derivative of the 918cc Morris Eight side-valve unit. Of this managerial mayhem, discussed more fully in Chapter Four, Daniels was unaware.

'The logic was to use the Wolseley Eight engine. But in the end this wasn't ever really considered — as the Minor was to replace the Series E, you just took the engine from that car.

'But just before the BMC merger . . . we were going to put the Wolseley ohv engine back into the Minor. I actually had a car running with that unit, and it was superb — a beautiful engine'.

Morris quality

'The subsequently installed 803cc A-Series engine wasn't really good enough, nor was the back axle, nor was the gearbox.

'You could bust the Austin gearbox in no time at all. The Morris box was a very strong, solid box – there was a lot of metal in it. The Austin gearbox was much lighter altogether. It used better-quality material, but although the Morris gearbox used lower-grade material there was a lot more of it – and as a result the Morris box was a damn sight quieter, too. The only thing with the Morris gearbox was that it used to jump out of second gear. It used to do that every time you tackled Porlock Hill. Morris had a bad name in Devon because of that gearbox . . .

'On the Minor we originally had a superb back axle, too. Yes, it was heavier than the Austin one, but it was more robust. I suppose you'd say it was over-engineered, as was the suspension – later we checked on some of these things, and I know now that I could have cut down the length of the torsion bars by a third, and they'd still have been perfectly adequate.

'When we were able to check a few things between ourselves and Austin, we discovered that we were getting our rear springs to do about 90,000 cycles while the Austin A30 ones gave us 14,000 cycles. That was the difference between us!

'The thing was that we'd decided we were going into the African market – the rough areas where no British car could live. They all went and had a go, and they came out pretty fast. We said, "We're going in, and we're going to stay there!" That's part of the reason why we over-engineered.'

The Traveller

At the same time as thought was being given to a new engine for the Minor, Nuffield engineers were also working

Jack Daniels (left) with his former colleague in the Minor design team, Reg Job, and a scale model of the original Mosquito. The MM is the first production Minor, and was restored by Morris apprentices as part of the 1961 celebrations for the millionth Minor. (Haymarket)

on additions to the Minor range – the van and pick-up, and the 'woody' Traveller.

'I didn't make the decision on the Traveller,' states Daniels. 'It was a mutual effort by "Issi" and the office body shop, I'd say. It was quite simply a result of the influence of America at the time. That was what the Americans were doing – wood-framed estate cars – and we had instructions to produce an estate, as a follow-up to the van.

'It was convenient to make the car that way, I know that. The wood part we could do in the Morris Bodies wood shop – it was easy to do, and at the time it was cost-effective. You had quite a lot of machining needed for the shaping of the woodwork, but it would have been achieved in the main by modifications to existing machinery.

And if you look at the metal panels, they weren't expensive.'

More experimental Minors

Around the time of the Wolseley-engined Minor, various other projects were embarked upon – including a Minor being fitted with Moulton rubber springing. The car used Alex Moulton's rubber-in-torsion 'Flexitor' units (rubber bonded between inner and outer steel tubes) at the front, and 'Rotoshear' discs of bonded rubber at the rear. The vehicle completed 1,000 trouble-free miles on MIRA's pavé, an important confirmation of the validity of rubber as a springing medium.

'There wasn't a metallic joint anywhere between the car's body and the suspension,' says Daniels. 'The sole

American influences were behind the Traveller's 'woody' construction, which Daniels says seemed cost-effective at the time. (Tony Baker/Classic & Sports Car)

objective was to reduce road noise. It didn't have the slightest effect, so it was abandoned.

'Still on the theme of road noise, we had a little shop in which we could do glass-fibre work, so we started to make glass-fibre panels – the bonnet, the doors, the bootlid, anything that was a "loose" panel – to see if we could reduce road noise by that means. But it did nothing for us, either . . .'

The front-wheel-drive Minor

Then there was the transverse-engined front-wheel-drive Minor, part-built when Issigonis left for Alvis in 1952 and completed soon after. 'The basic thought behind the whole thing,' confirms Daniels, 'was to find means of getting more payload space in the same size vehicle. This was the idea behind Issigonis's thinking all the time – and the car was very much his idea.'

The gearbox was end-on, and at the hub end the drive was through a cross between a conventional Hooke joint and a specially hardened sliding Cardan joint. This made for a bulky hub assembly.

'It was quite a long time before we came up with the solution we did, but in the end it worked all right,' says Daniels. 'There was quite a lot of steering fight, though. We couldn't get the joint far out enough – the ideal is to get the middle of the universal joint down the axis of the kingpin, as Citroën did with the DS, and then you have absolutely ideal geometry.

'I actually used the car for two or three years as my personal transport. When I was asked in 1956 to join Issigonis at Longbridge I could have borrowed anything I wanted from Cowley. But it was winter, and there was a lot of snow about, so I took the fwd Minor as a hack. The ability of that car to operate uphill, on snow – that's what really got me about it.

'I also remember taking it to Silverstone. It had a column gearchange – it was convenient to do, and worked very well – and that's what people must have spotted. Because when I got back to the car there were lots of people on their knees in the mud, peering underneath. Alec would have been a bit cross if he'd known.'

Further experiments with suspension

Suspension on the fwd Minor was perfectly ordinary – the standard torsion bar set-up at the front and a simple leaf-sprung (Lancia-style) dead axle at the rear: hardly surprising, perhaps, on a car intended essentially to test an engine/transmission configuration and nothing more. But that's not to say that thoughts on the Minor's suspension stopped dead with the discarding of the torsion bar rear or the abandoning of the Moulton experiments. Indeed not – in the mid-1950s Issigonis's team looked at coil springs and struts for the front of the Minor.

'We gave up on the struts, largely because cornering ability was in our opinion bloody dangerous. When you took a corner, transverse forces acting on the strut bearing caused a friction lock-up, and the vehicle just didn't roll at all. People weren't conscious of the speed at which they were taking corners, and they just lost control.'

Independent rear suspension

Rather later in the life of the Minor, Daniels devised for it an independent rear suspension, using semi-trailing arms and what he terms 'VW-type springs' – transverse leaves operating as a laminated torsion bar.

'It was dead easy to do. The floor by the rear heelboard and forward spring-hanger area came up at an angle that just happened to be absolutely right. Using the spring-hangers and a couple of brackets, the suspension could be bolted straight on, and the suspension

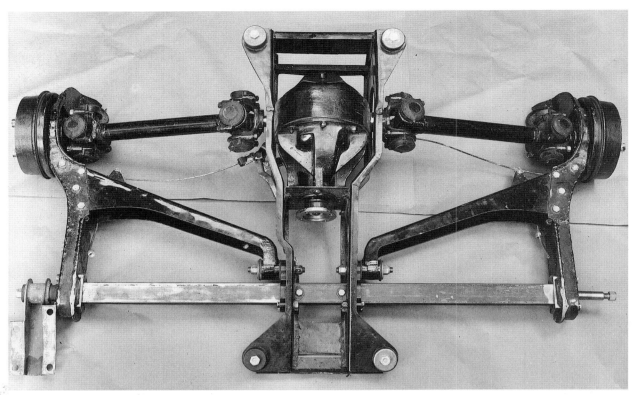

The independent rear suspension Daniels devised for the Minor used semi-trailing arms and a square-section torsion bar. Clearly visible here are the Moulton rubber universal joints used inboard and outboard. (BMIHT/Rover)

arms ended up at pretty much the correct angle, with just a hint of a semi-trailing attitude.'

The suspension used Mouton rubber universal joints both inboard and outboard, and the differential housing was one of a batch still in store, according to Daniels, having been commissioned in the mid-'30s for use on an independently sprung MG — presumably the R-type racer. Two more were pulled off the shelf in the 1960s when he wanted a differential housing for a couple of four-wheel-drive Mini-Moke prototypes then being built.

'We didn't do much experimenting with the irs Minor,' says Daniels. 'I was impressed by it. But it didn't survive — the cost counted against it.'

So the Minor lived on until 1971 largely unchanged — although, as Daniels recalls, 'it was nearly stopped several times'. When Issigonis returned to BMC in 1956, after his brief spell at Alvis, Daniels joined him at his new base in Longbridge. As the two of them worked first on the experimental Moulton-suspended 1.5-litre XC9001, then on what ultimately became the 1100, and as they eventually threw their all into the Mini, the Minor became past history for them.

A spread of the earliest catalogues for the Minor. The single-sheet mono catalogue (top right) features what are almost certainly two pre-production cars; the tourer, registration NWL 433, has a 'D' lamp to illuminate the number plate, and a single-piece rear bumper, neither of which featured on production cars. It is probably an export-only printing. The two white-covered catalogues are internally the same, but have different covers. Top left is an earlier printing, dated 8/48 for the home market and 1/49 for the US version; cars in the latter retain right-hand-drive. The later export catalogue (bottom right) is in English, French and Spanish and is dated 9/48. The black-covered catalogue is for the US, and dated 4/49. All these catalogues feature colour artwork with charming subsidiary images, plus mono photos on the specification pages.

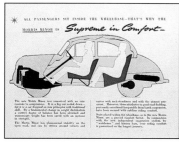

The original white-covered Minor catalogues launched the slogan 'The World's Supreme Small Car'. Note the one-piece rear bumper on the saloon, and the matching recessed rear light and reflector; other shots show a divided front bumper without the painted bridging plate of production cars.

This early US-market catalogue, dated 4/49, has a new black cover, extra pages, and features cars with US-legal raised headlamps. 'Enjoy the new Lull-abye Ride in the MORRIS!' runs the copy on one page. The artwork is new, with left-hand-drive cars, the correct production bumper configuration, the later triangular rear lamps, and the correct boot badge. Interestingly, the main images of the tourer lack trafficators.

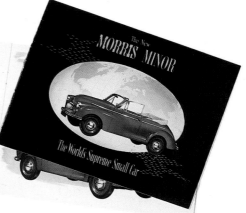

This double-page spread (bottom) is from the same catalogue, and extols 'the phenomenal power output of the MORRIS MINOR husky British Bulldog engine'.

These early full Morris range catalogues both date from July 1949, are in standard-size landscape format, and feature Minor, 'MO' Oxford and 'MS' Six. The catalogue with the black cover is in Danish, while the cream-covered catalogue is in English.

Contents of the two 1949 range catalogues are essentially the same, with coloured artwork predominant, but two pages of mono photos of the Oxford in the Nuffield test chambers, and mono photos to illustrate the radio fittings on the Oxford/Six.

The colours change on the two-page main spread for the Minor, with the British-market saloon becoming a darker green and the tourer changing from black in the Danish catalogue to maroon for the home-market publication.

This small-format catalogue for the 1950 Morris range, with 10/49 dating, has a horizontal 'landscape' presentation, and features re-touched mono photos against a pale green background. The single sheet unfolds to give a centre spread of the three cars. Shown are English and Dutch versions.

This four-page supplementary catalogue, dated 7/50, was published for the 1950 Motor Show launch of the four-door Minor saloon. Inside are mono photos.

This small-format catalogue for the 1951 Morris range, dated 8/50, is a single sheet folding to 8¹/2 x 5¹/2 inches; it unfolds to give a poster-format centre spread of the three-car range. The first spread, as the catalogue opens, promotes the new four-door Minor, 'available for export only'. Colour artwork is used, with a spread of colour-tinted mono photos to illustrate particular features. Shown are English and Dutch variants.

This undated landscape-format 8¹/2 x 5¹/2 inch US catalogue for the Minor features mono photos (that of the front suspension is upside-down) on a yellow background, and unfolds to 11 x 17 inches. The open car now has integral glass rear side-windows, and the grille is painted, but the engine remains the 918cc side-valve for all models, so the catalogue must have been current between June 1951 and July 1952.

The particularly fine Morris range catalogue for 1952 – dated 9/51 – is in vertical 'portrait' format, with the slogan 'Morris "Quality First" establishes a new class in economy motoring'. Typefaces are now more modern, and the catalogue mixes colour artwork, line drawings (taken from photos) with spot colour, and mono and colourised mono photography. Each model has a double-page colour-artwork spread, and another double-page spread emphasises the virtues of 'Monoconstruction'.

Chapter Three

The flat-four engine

I T'S WELL-KNOWN that the Minor was designed around a flat-four engine. The cast-iron unit was intended to be made in two capacities — 800cc and 1100cc — and it had side valves; that too is well-known. This, however, is about as far as most people go: there are no known photographs of the flat-four, and most of those involved with the design and construction of the engine are now dead.

As a consequence there is a distressing lack of information about a component at the heart of the Minor's design. So what, if anything, can be gleaned today about this relatively short-lived experiment?

Why a flat-four?

A horizontally opposed or 'boxer' engine has the basic characteristic of being smoother and better-balanced than an in-line engine. This is because having cylinders opposite each other means that the firing forces balance each other out.

A more fundamental advantage is the compactness of a horizontally opposed engine. As a result, because the engine is shorter, the crankshaft is more rigid and so is the crankcase. This is a straightforward design benefit, as is the lower centre of gravity conferred on the car by the engine being less tall than an in-line unit.

Every bit as valuable, however, is the fact that a compact engine configuration means that the power unit takes up less space within the vehicle. This is the nub of the matter: for Issigonis few things were more important than space-efficient packaging. 'His thoughts were always to keep down the amount of space taken up by the engine,' recalls Jack Daniels. 'He wanted it to be as compact as possible, because he was after maximum body space.'

The packaging advantages of a flat-four are graphically illustrated in a trio of line drawings dated 1944. These

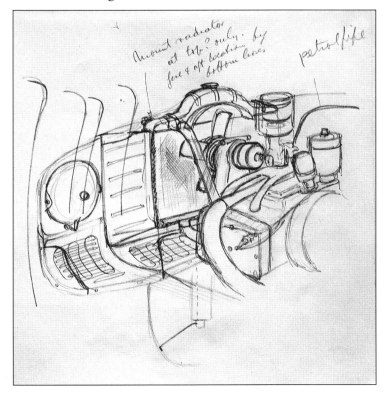

This early Issigonis sketch of the flat-four installation shows the compactness of this type of engine. The vertical starter is clearly visible. (BMIHT/Rover)

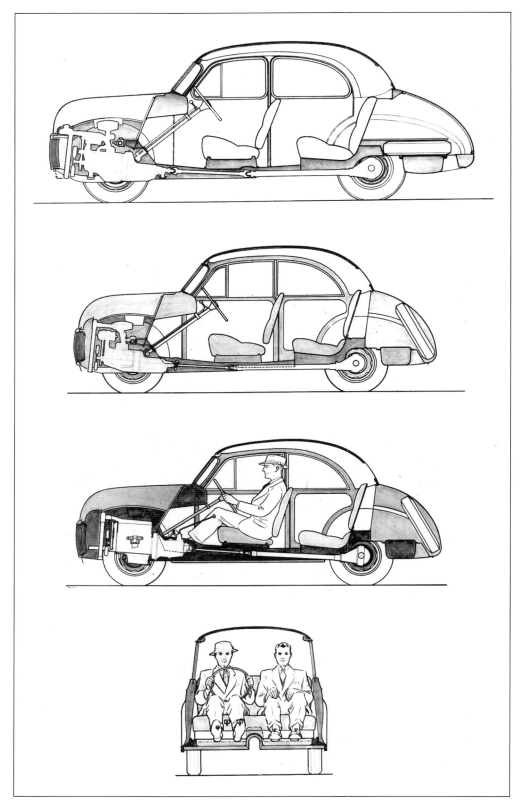

These packaging drawings from 1944 eloquently demonstrate the space-saving advantages of the flat-four. At the top is an 'Intermediate' saloon of Oxford size, with a flat-four; below is a flat-four Mosquito; and finally, at the bottom, a Mosquito with a conventional in-line engine and normal gearbox. The extra front-footboard space and the shorter bonnet of the flat-four Mosquito is clearly depicted. Notice how all three cars use torque-tube transmission in conjunction with a split propshaft. (BMIHT/Rover)

depict an Oxford-sized car with a flat-four engine, and two Mosquitoes, one with a conventional in-line engine and one with a flat-four. The latter has the engine mounted further forward (also giving more secure handling), a compact gearbox limiting transmission intrusion into the passenger compartment, and a shorter bonnet. A torque-tube rear axle is used, and the low-down mounting of the flat-four is shown as allowing the split propshaft to operate at a shallower angle and the torque-tube to lie flat rather than at a space-encroaching angle.

These are important drawings, as they hint at several design characteristics of the Issigonis flat-four power pack – including the torque-tube rear axle, which was indeed used on the first 'try-out' Mosquito prototype.

Three different capacities

As originally conceived, the Mosquito was to be a smaller car than the 8hp Series E. This was clearly laid out at a February 1944 meeting called 'to determine the basic car production policy in the immediate and early post-war periods of reconstruction'. At this important meeting it was determined that there would be three post-war Morris models: a Mosquito, a Minor, and a 1½-litre or 1¾-litre Major. This was, of course, rather different from the Minor, Oxford and Morris Six trio ultimately announced at the 1948 Motor Show. The descriptions of the Mosquito and Minor make fascinating reading.

'. . . the first of the series should be a chassis-less two-seater with occasional seating for four, non-opening boot, fixed screen, of the general design of car produced in Mr Issigonis's experimental shop, and known as the Mosquito. This will be fitted with either a flat-four, flat-twin, or four-cylinder in-line engine of approximately 750cc according to the results obtained from experimental

engines now under construction.

'The second of the series would be a chassis-less four-seater family car, in effect a modernised version of the present 8hp car, giving slightly more body accommodation, but by reason of the incorporation of a flat-four-cylinder engine of approximately 1100cc and by using torsion-bar suspension and a modern four-light layout, would be lighter and more economical . . .'

In other words, an 1100cc flat-four Minor to replace the Eight was in the picture almost from the start, and the Mosquito as conceived by Issigonis and his team was to slot below such a car. The first Mosquito prototype was indeed essentially a three-seater, with no rear seat but a front bench spacious enough – as Jack Daniels testifies – for three people.

Although this first car was initially powered by a Morris Eight engine, it was designed to take the flat-four, and at this stage it was seen as being a 6hp unit. This is confirmed by the experimental model code given to the first six pre-production prototypes. This was EX/SX, followed by the car number, with the first car being EX/SX/86. The 'SX' prefix stood simply for SiX horse-power.

To qualify as a 6hp for tax purposes the engine would have been smaller than 800cc, which would then have equated to a 7hp or 8hp rating. Assuming that a 6hp would have a stroke no longer than 75mm, the maximum bore size allowable under the RAC horsepower formula would be 49.5mm, giving a capacity of 577cc. That's the size of a Fiat Topolino engine, give or take a cubic centimetre or two, and ties in well with the notion of a two-seater runabout.

But what's all that about flat-twins and small in-line engines? It's not pie in the sky. At the end of 1943 Morris Motors Engines Branch was directed to build a flat-twin, a 'four-cylinder in-line

49mm bore engine' and 'one four-cylinder horizontally opposed 700cc engine'.

Was the flat-twin built? Perhaps it was, perhaps it wasn't. But the in-line engine was definitely built, and is evidence of the size the Mosquito was intended to be — small enough to be powered by a 6hp unit of no more than 600cc. This engine was coded the 'BSFM', had a special lightweight gear-box designed and made for it, and is referred to in a 1946 Morris memo as 'the 600cc side-valve job'. So it happened — and is proof that even at this early stage Morris was hedging its bets on the type of power unit for its envisaged 6hp car.

So far, then, we have confirmation that three capacities for the flat-four were at one time or another studied: 700cc (and thus no longer 6hp!), 800cc, and 1100cc. This is borne out by minutes of the 14 April 1947 Morris

---

The eight pre-production Mosquito/Minor prototypes

Experimental no	Build date	Engine
EX/SX/86	1.12.43	Not recorded
EX/SX/130	29.8.46	Not recorded
EX/SX/131	29.8.46	Not recorded
EX/SX/132	21.1.47	Apparently 918cc SV in-line
EX/SX/133	27.1.47	800cc flat-four
EX/SX/134	3.4.47	1100cc flat-four
EX/SMM/144	14.6.48	918cc SV in-line
EX/SMM/145	2.9.48	918cc SV in-line

All but EX/SX/132 are two-door saloons; EX/SX/132 is a Tourer. Build dates are not necessarily the date of completion, and are more likely to be the date when the car was allocated its EX number.

---

board meeting. These record vice-chairman Sir Miles Thomas as saying that since the Mosquito's conception in 1941 the engine size had twice been increased — in other words once to 800cc and a second time to 1100cc.

Was the '6hp' flat-four ever built? Jack Daniels has no recollections at all

of such an engine, and what little evidence there is would seem to confirm that this small-capacity unit was not made.

The first flat-four engine was apparently built during spring and summer 1945, judging by correspondence between Sir Miles Thomas and Morris Engines. In April 1945 it was not yet complete, because of certain casting problems. By September, however, Thomas was able to write of 'the prototype Mosquito, which is now fitted with a flat-four engine and a one-piece propeller shaft'.

This engine was almost certainly of 800cc. The proof? A note from Morris director H. Seaward to Vic Oak, headed 'Mosquito' and dated 2 February 1945. 'This memorandum,' Seaward wrote, 'is to confirm the agreement arrived at this afternoon, namely to install the flat-four 800cc engine in the above car.'

Given that two months later Engine Branch was still struggling to build what one assumes is the first flat-four, the decision to go for an 800cc unit came early enough for the engine to be built to this capacity from the start.

Moving beyond this, we know both 800cc and 1100cc versions were completed. We know from Experimental Department records (see the accompanying table) that an 800cc engine was fitted to the fifth pre-production prototype, EX/SX/133, which has a build date of 27 January 1947. The records also confirm that an 1100cc version was fitted into the next prototype, EX/SX/134, which has a build date of 3 April 1947.

So why the different capacities? The 6hp was clearly a response to the perceived role of the Mosquito as a small runabout to slot below the Morris Eight. With the horsepower tax rising from 15 shillings to 25 shillings per horsepower in 1940, the idea of a smaller car than the Morris Eight clearly had an appeal. Ultimately, though, this was abandoned when it was evident that concentrating on a four-seater replacement for the Eight would be a more viable proposition.

In this larger format the 800cc flat-four would give adequate power while attracting a suitably low rate of taxation under the then prevailing tax by fiscal horsepower. Overseas markets, not trammelled by a tax-by-horsepower and more appreciative of greater engine power, would get the 1100cc unit; the 800cc version would, however, be an option in export markets, as boardroom minutes confirm.

How many engines were built?

From the completion of the first Mosquito prototype to the axing of the flat-four programme in June 1947, the flat-four was in the picture for three and a half years. It is reasonable to assume that fair numbers of the power unit were built, but such an assumption may not be safe.

'I only saw about three engines altogether. They may have had more at Morris Engines in Coventry, but they never arrived at Cowley,' says Jack Daniels. 'I can't remember whether there were two 1100cc engines and one 800cc, or two 800cc engines and one 1100cc. But we would have had one car with each and had the third engine running on a test-bed. There were never six prototypes with the flat-four.'

The memories of Eric Hill, who in 1946 was a fitter in the Morris Engines toolroom, go some way to corroborating the recollections of Daniels. Most of the work on experimental engines would have passed through the toolroom, says Hill, and he himself recalls working in 1946 on three flat-four blocks – drilling holes, tapping, and drilling out oil holes – over a period of several weeks. A particular memory is of how small and easy to handle were the engine blocks.

'If more engines had been made I'd have known about it — at least if they'd been done at Morris Engines,' says Hill. 'If they'd been done outside, I wouldn't have known'.

We know that at least one engine had been built in 1945. However, Morris board minutes for 7 May 1946 record the head of Engines Branch as promising 'to push forward with the production of prototype test engines for the Mosquito', these quite likely being the engines Eric Hill recalls. Crucially, the implication is that by this date very little else had been built. Certainly, the first mention in Experimental Department records of a prototype with a flat-four is the entry referring to EX/SX/133, with its January 1947 build date. It is thus plausible that the two prototypes built during summer 1946 at first either had to make do with a single flat-four engine between them – this being the first engine, built in 1945 – or else use a Morris Eight power unit as a temporary expedient.

Whether or not this is the case, there remains the question of whether more flat-fours were built after the three-engine batch Hill recalls. There is some evidence to suggest that, amid the confusions of a troubled 1947, manufacture of further engines stalled. Certainly at the 2 January 1947 Morris board meeting Vic Oak was recorded as saying that 'at least three production-type engines were urgently required for road testing'; the implication is that up until that point all that had been supplied were prototype/experimental engines.

In the six months up until the June 1947 cancellation of the flat-four, Morris Engines was endeavouring, possibly without much enthusiasm, to produce the first prototypes of the bigger 1300cc and 1500cc flat-four engines intended for the Oxford. This was a project that was evidently dragging its feet and that would ultimately come to nothing, with the Oxford instead being given a 1476cc side-valve in-line engine.

It was also a time when the Mosquito looked as if it might have its place taken by an MG or Wolseley derivative powered by an in-line ohc engine. In such circumstances it is quite conceivable that at an over-worked Morris Engines Branch no more Mosquito flat-fours were produced after the 1946 batch of three.

A definite conclusion is not possible, though. In particular, John Barker, then an apprentice in the experimental department at Morris Engines, recalls destroying a batch of flat-four engines in the 1949/50 period — dismantling the power units, then sawing them up. 'There were four or five of them, something like that — certainly more than two or three,' he says.

Two different engines

What were the design characteristics of the Mosquito flat-four? Here there are as many mysteries and imponderables as elsewhere. There is, however, some documentary evidence to go on, not least a series of Morris engineering drawings dating from 1946. Fascinatingly, these depict two different versions of the engine, one called the YF80M and the other the ZF80M.

Were both made? A possible clue is that Mosquito prototype EX/SX/133 is recorded as having an 800cc YF80M engine, while EX/SX/134 is listed as having an 1100cc YF11M unit. No other flat-four engine numbers are given in the Morris records concerning the Mosquito prototypes. But that does not necessarily mean that only 'Y-type' engines were built.

The flat-four with the dry sump

The most startling feature of the ZF80M is that it is clearly a dry-sump design, with two pumps and no oil pan. This race-car technology involves having a separate oil tank, and the use of one pump to distribute oil to the bearings and a second 'scavenge' pump to pump it back to the tank. Why use such an expensive solution? The obvious answer is that it enables the engine to be less high, thereby lowering even further the car's centre of gravity. Was a dry-sump engine built, though?

'I know we did something with dry sumps, but I can't place it,' says Jack Daniels. He does, however, admit that Issigonis would quite likely have considered a dry sump as a way of keeping the engine weight low down in the car. Indeed, the flat-four depicted in the 1944 packaging drawings looks so remarkably compact that it may well have been drawn as a dry-sump unit.

Confirmation that a dry-sump engine must have been made comes from a 30 August 1945 note from Jack Shaw of Engines Branch to Sir Miles Thomas. This memo tells Thomas that 'we are revising the design of the flat-four to eliminate the scavenge pump, etc, and consequently a new specification has had to be pieced together'.

Given that the first 'try-out' Mosquito prototype was running around with a flat-four ten days later, there's no way that the conversion to a wet sump spoken of by Shaw could have been incorporated into that particular engine within those ten days. Conclusion: at least one dry-sump flat-four was tested in the Mosquito.

Angled cylinder heads

Another oddity of the ZF80M is the way the cylinder heads are angled downwards, as a result of a diagonal face to the top of each bank of cylinders. This is peculiar, to say the least, and suggests a large wedge-shaped combustion chamber in the bore itself.

'I can't remember the blocks being sloping like that,' says Daniels. 'I wouldn't raise any objections against it, though. Go back to MG, and H. N. Charles had a theory that you ought to be able to arrange the piston with a

End views of the ZF80M engine, dated June 1946, show how extremely shallow it is. Look closer, and the reason is apparent: there are two oil pumps, and no conventional oil pan. In these views the vertical starter can also be seen, along with the lack of any water inlets on the cylinder heads. Most striking, though, is the angle of the cylinder heads. (BMIHT/Rover)

slope, so that it actually pushed the flame front forward during combustion. He tried it on the MG overhead-cam engine and it jolly well worked. I don't think Issigonis would have pinched the idea from H. N. Charles, but Charles was at Cowley at around that time, so he may have been an influence.

'I'm sure, though, that the blocks on the engines we saw had two parallel faces, so that in machining it you could pass them through two cutters at the same time. I'm not sure you could do that if you had the faces angled.'

It's also worth noting that the ZF80M appears not to have any water inlets on the cylinder heads, making do instead with an inlet and an outlet on each forward face of the block. With the dry-sump system giving the oil an enhanced role in cooling the engine, and with the combustion chambers situated in the cylinder bores, perhaps the heads were felt to need less extensive cooling.

It's hard to imagine cost-accountants feeling enthusiastic about the ZF80M's elaborate engineering solutions. This was a power unit intended for a cheap car, and Morris was no Citroën. Unsurprisingly, YF80M is altogether more orthodox, with a single oil pump, a wet sump, and straightforward flat cylinder block faces.

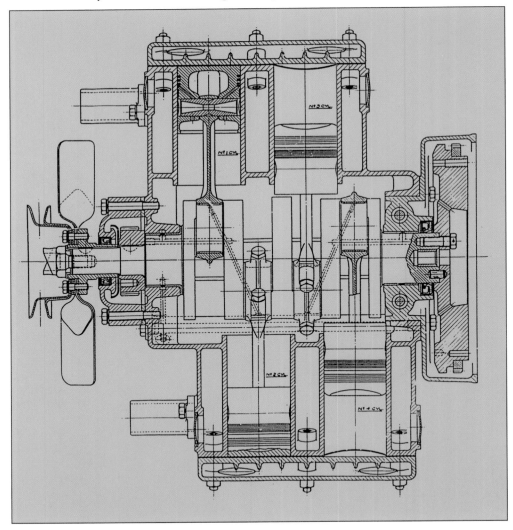

The sectional plan through the crankshaft centreline shows that the ZF80M pistons have a recessed bowl. (BMIHT/Rover)

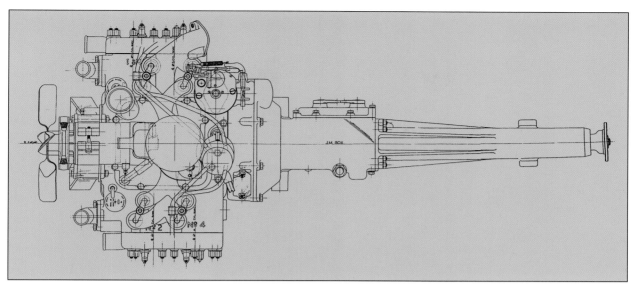

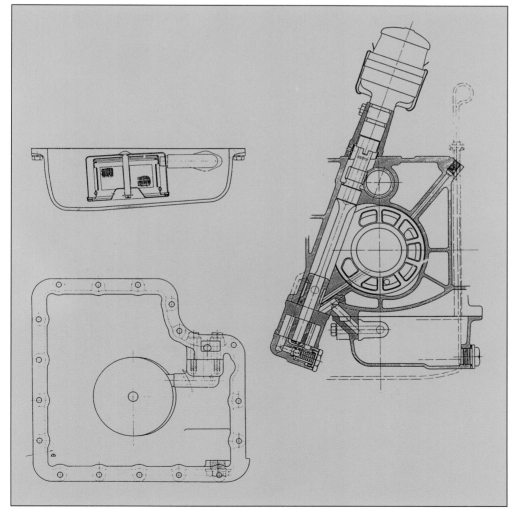

In plan view the YF80M is a very different animal. The heads appear to have water inlets, and the gearbox is a compact unit with side selectors and a long tailshaft. The later is a gauge of how far forward the short flat-four would have been mounted. (BMIHT/Rover)

The YF80M marks a return to a conventional sump. This sectional drawing shows the orthodox auxiliary drive off the camshaft, with a shaft driving the oil pump at one end and the distributor at the other. Unusually, though, the oil pump is situated outside the sump. This is the only surviving engineering drawing to mention the 1100cc YF11M engine. (BMIHT/Rover)

The crankshaft: two main bearings

The crankshaft of the Mosquito flat-four always had two main bearings. With the shorter crank of a flat-four this isn't necessarily a disadvantage, if the mains are sufficiently beefy — and to add a centre bearing would be to increase the length of the engine. Daniels states that the crankshaft had generously proportioned mains and never gave any problems. Interestingly, the side-valve flat-four Steyr engine, of which Issigonis cannot have been unaware, used three main bearings.

A vertical starter

Dominating the cross-section of both engines is the vertical position of the starter motor, with the Bendix on an auxiliary shaft driven by a bevel gear. This might seem a tortuous way of mounting a starter, and it would have added to costs, since a special starter motor would have had to be supplied by Lucas. However, the tightly packed lower reaches of the Mosquito engine-bay seemingly precluded any other arrangement.

'It was the most convenient place

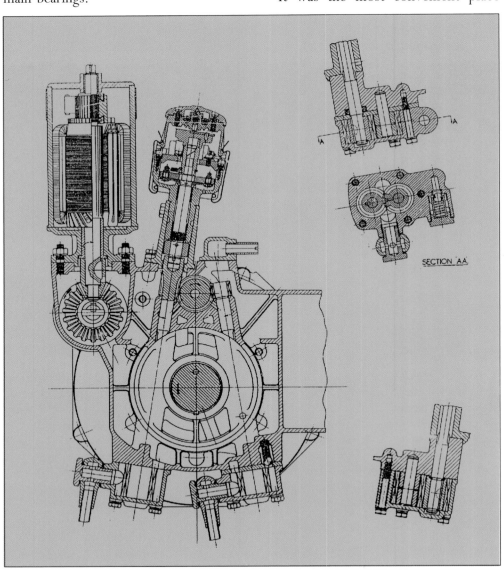

In cross-section the ZF's two pumps are clearly shown, along with the bevel drive for the starter Bendix. (BMIHT/Rover)

SECTION A.A.

SECTION AAA.

The vertical starter operates the Bendix via a bevel-drive auxiliary shaft. (BMIHT/Rover)

to put the starter, and it worked all right – we never had any trouble with it,' says Daniels, who recalls that at one stage a mechanical system of engagement was used, pushing the Bendix into engagement manually with a lever.

Gear drive for the camshaft

In common with most of the Wolseley-derived overhead-cam engines previously used by the Nuffield Organisation, Issigonis eschewed chain drive of the camshaft in favour of gears. In this instance the drive was direct, whereas on the gear-driven Wolseley engines a shaft-and-bevel arrangement was used. Simplicity and silence would have been the main benefits. Daniels has no specific recollections of the camshaft drive. 'Whatever way we did it, it would have been because it was the most convenient,' he says.

Second thoughts on auxiliary drives?

An early Issigonis sketch of the flat-four shows the distributor and oil-pump drives being taken off the front of the engine, via a helical gear on the crankshaft. This is an odd idea. On the YF80M and ZF80M engineering drawings it is, however, clear that the auxiliary drives are taken off the rear of the camshaft. This altogether more orthodox arrangement ties in with another and presumably later Issigonis sketch.

Another apparent change of heart concerns the fan position. On the ZF80M the fan is mounted on the crankshaft pulley, whereas on the YF80M – and on the second sketch – the fan is mounted in more regular fashion on the end of the dynamo.

Downdraught carburation

On the plan view of the YF80M the use

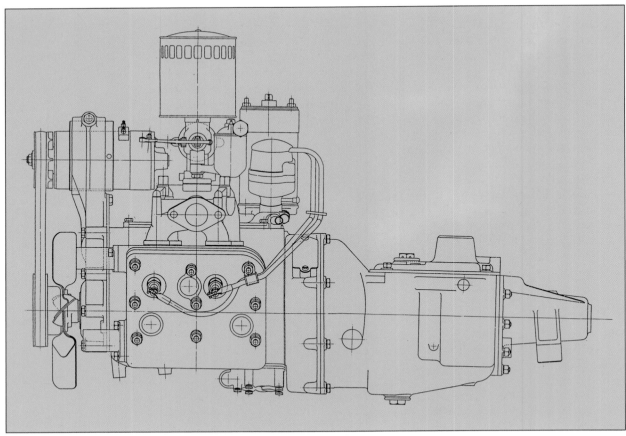

of a downdraught SU — with the carb body lying flat — is clearly visible. This was an arrangement favoured on various Nuffield cars, and has the advantage of feeding the mixture straight into the manifold. But Daniels recalls that on the flat-four it didn't result in a very happy fuel delivery — although he can't remember exactly the nature of the shortcomings.

Manifolding is looked after by a combined inlet and exhaust manifold in the form of an 'H'; underneath are two removable covers giving access to the tappets.

A compact transmission

Certainly the engine was physically small — perhaps 12–14 inches from the crankshaft pulley to the flywheel, according to John Barker. It was also relatively light, Morris Engines giving a figure of

181lb for the 800cc flat-four, against 195lb for the Morris Eight engine.

Equally compact was the gearbox. Comprehensively redesigned by Jack Daniels, this was initially a three-speeder, using Morris Eight Series II parts. Ultimately, however, a four-speed unit was used.

'The original Mosquito gearbox was basically Morris Eight, but the control mechanism wasn't standard. The external dimensions were cut down to the minimum possible,' says Daniels. 'We wrapped the casing as tight as we could around the mechanism, and we gained a lot of space by abandoning the actuating rods inside the box in favour of rotary levers through the side of the casing, coupling these to a simple column-change system. It all worked very well — in fact it was one of the exceptional column changes of the time. It really was a good one.'

One consequence of the compact gearbox and the forward positioning of the engine was that the distance between gearbox and back axle was considerable. On the 1944 packaging drawings referred to earlier, a split propshaft and a torque tube were depicted, the latter almost certainly being envisaged in conjunction with torsion-bar rear springing. By the time of the 1946 engine drawings, however, a different solution had been adopted. This was a substantial tailshaft on the gearbox, allowing a short conventional propshaft to be used. Doubtless this was more cost-effective, but it would have meant some loss of space in the front passenger compartment.

Driving the flat-four

Did it work? That's the only question that really matters. It's well known that there were problems with vibration, caused, says Daniels, by a poorly located flywheel; this is discussed fully in Chapter Two. The vibration was still an issue in April 1947, when Miles Thomas told the Morris board that although the flat-four was proving reliable, the vibration problems had been only 'temporarily overcome', and their complete eradication when the engine was worn could not be guaranteed.

That apart, the verdict was mixed. 'It should have been quite ideal,' says Jack Daniels. 'We tested mainly the 1100, and that gave reasonable performance – certainly much better than the Morris Eight engine. It was actually pretty good. You were conscious of a typical flat-four exhaust beat – it all seemed a bit off-key, and different from any other engine – but you got used to it.'

Fred Collis, a former employee of Morris Engines, recalls two cars with the flat-four engine, and remembers his father driving one of them from Coventry to Cowley. 'He said the car was marvellous, and had far more speed than a Morris Eight. He was very impressed by the performance.'

Nuffield engineer Jim Lambert was in his early 20s at the time, and all he knew about the flat-four was second-hand. But what he heard was less rosy. 'I don't think it ever had a chance. It was gutless, from what I gathered. It wasn't any real advance on what we had – it certainly wasn't a big step forward, such as from the A-series to the Rover Group K-series.'

In compensation there were, however, the benefits conferred on chassis behaviour by the use of the flat-four, as Daniels stresses:

'With the flat-four, the suspension was as ideal as you could possibly make it, in terms of geometry. When we had to fit the Morris Eight engine we were determined not to give way on our steering geometry one bit. We had to lift the engine up, but we didn't want to lift the steering with it, because it

---

The four-speed Mosquito gearbox

The change to a four-speed gearbox was written into the Mosquito specification in September 1946, at which stage the making of patterns and dies for the three-speed box was already well advanced.

Faced with this policy change, Engines Branch's first fear was that the Eight-derived three-speeder might become too heavy if converted to four speeds. As a consequence it looked at adapting the lightweight four-speed gearbox it had designed for the 600cc side-valve 'BSFM' engine.

The snag was that this box was judged too feeble to cope with the 1100cc flat-four. This meant that a second new gearbox might have to be built, suitable for the bigger Mosquito engine and for the Oxford's projected flat-fours. In addition, the 'BSFM' gearbox had no synchromesh on second gear, an omission that caused some concern: unless synchromesh could be schemed in, there was a risk of customer resistance to a 'crash' second. Yet the edict was for the new Mosquito four-speeder to be as cheap to make as possible . . .

The first four-speed gearboxes were apparently delivered to Cowley as late as April 1947. What solution was ultimately used is not known, but faced with such complications, Engines Branch doubtless had another reason to breathe a sigh of relief when the flat-four was cancelled.

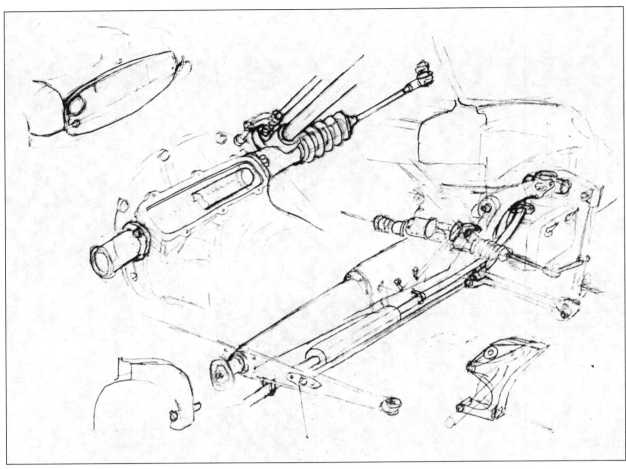

was in the ideal location. So I dared, with much trepidation, to cut a hole in the top of the bellhousing, so we could lift the gearbox while maintaining the steering unchanged.'

In a way this was a return, in fact, to a scheme sketched out by Issigonis at an earlier stage in the Mosquito's development. With typical economy of thought, he envisaged slotting the rack through the bellhousing, to achieve a position for it that was as low as possible. As far as Daniels can recall, this bold notion was never actually tried.

Why the flat-four was canned

The opinion of Jack Daniels is straight-forward: the flat-four was dropped because the vibration problem caused by the poorly located flywheel wasn't solved in time. Former Morris Engines man John Barker, however, was told at the time that there were other failings.

'Engineers in the Experimental Department said that it had died the death because of bearing trouble — the bearings were too noisy. The explanation I was given was that there was crankshaft whip. I could easily believe this was because with only two main bearings there was not enough support for the crankshaft.'

This could well have been the case. Equally, any tendency for the crankshaft to whip in extreme circumstances could have been exacerbated by vibration generated by an out-of-true or loosely fixed flywheel. These are the sort of problems that development would normally have ironed out fairly quickly —

had time, resources and management goodwill allowed.

Over and above such basic engineering considerations, there was also the dislike of the grumpily conservative Lord Nuffield for any fancy engine, says Daniels.

'Nuffield said, "You can have any engine you like so long as it's already in production." This led us to the Morris Eight engine. He wouldn't even let us put in the ohv Wolseley version, which we wanted to use. He wanted the Morris to be side-valve – he was a side-valve man, full stop.'

It wasn't that simple, though. The flat-four was going to be an expensive engine to produce. Figures survive to confirm this. In July 1947 it was calculated that the YF80M and its special gearbox would cost £47 3s 0d to manufacture; the Morris Eight engine and gearbox, in contrast, was costed at £38 – making the flat-four a whacking 24 per cent more expensive. In fairness, the Wolseley Eight ohv engine and its Morris Eight gearbox was costed up at £52, but that doesn't detract from the very real cost implications of going for the flat-four.

Worse, as far as the Morris Engines Branch was concerned it 'wasn't invented here'. Struggling to put Tom Brown's family of in-line power units into production, Courthouse Green can only have regarded the flat-four as a cuckoo in an already overcrowded nest.

Let's throw something more into the pot. In the aircraft industry it was widely accepted at the time that you never arranged to have two unknowns in the equation. If you had a new airframe, you wouldn't use a new engine at the same time: that way you risked having two sets of development problems. The same principle applies in the motor business. The Mosquito, as it was then, was a radical new design – so radical that management was demonstrably unsure about its prospects. Dial in a freaky all-new flat-four engine and

you can understand why the guys in grey felt a bit shaky about the whole thing.

Not only that, but the development of the Mosquito flat-four had dragged on. In June 1946 it had been expected that the engine would be in production before mid-1947, yet in April '47 they were still fretting about the unsolved vibration problem. And there had always been doubts about the unit.

Why the flat-four cost so much

At one stage Morris Engines itemised those features of the flat-four that added to its manufacturing cost. They were listed as: special manifolds; bevel starter drive; separate flywheel housing to permit crank assembly; separate tappet carrier; cast tappet cover for rigidity; longer valves and tappets; eccentric dynamo mounting in timing case; gear drive instead of chain drive to camshaft; external oil pump requiring separate suction unit in the sump; four water connections when there was only one on the Morris Eight engine.

As early as 1944 there was hesitation. The relevant passages from the minutes of the 2 February 1944 Nuffield board meeting speak for themselves:

'. . . it was decided that although development work might well still continue on the flat-four engine then envisaged, it was considered desirable that a four-cylinder in-line power unit should be incorporated in the Mosquito series and that suitable development work on engines should forthwith begin in this connection.'

By early January 1947 there were still no 'production-type' Mosquito flat-fours, and there was talk of the intended 1300cc/1500cc flat-fours for the Oxford being abandoned, to simplify production at Morris Engines. In the end it was decided in late January to keep the Oxford flat-four – although the decision was subsequently reversed. The argument was that the bigger flat-four – interestingly, if implausibly –

would be cheaper to make than an in-line engine, and that adapting the body to an in-line engine would incur extra costs. But clearly the idea of horizontally opposed engines was under attack.

The decisive blow came at the 24 June 1947 Morris board meeting:

'The vice-chairman stated that a flat rate tax of £10 had made it necessary to reconsider the forward programme of models. It was desirable that fewer types be produced by the Organisation, and it was considered that high-priced small cars would not be popular unless their performance offered outstanding attrac-

tion . . . Flat-four engines would be deleted from the production programme, resulting in engine manufacture being greatly simplified. Development work on the flat-fours in Coventry, however, would not be abandoned.'

But it was. Logic, fed by internal pressures from Tom Brown and his Engines Branch team, had prevailed. Given the chaotic industrial, economic and managerial situations prevailing in 1947 — surely one of the most wretched years in Britain's post-war history — such a decision is understandable. It's a shame, all the same.

Chapter Four

The Minors that never were

MUCH OF THE appeal of the Morris Minor lies, it seems, in how little it changed during its 23-year life. That was never how it was intended. Indeed, there would almost certainly have been a completely re-bodied Minor by the mid-1950s at the latest, had Morris designers had their way. Just as fascinating, though, are all the experimental Minors created — or merely contemplated — over the years.

And some of these you'll never have heard of before . . .

Nearly launched as a Wolseley . . .

Before tooling delays put back the programme, the Mosquito, as it was then called, was originally to have been launched in January 1947, as a two-door with the flat-four engine. A four-door and a Wolseley version were to

Wolseley 'Wasp' mock-up, 1947: note the sliding roof, then being considered as an option, and – just visible – a horn ring on the steering wheel. What the bumpers would have been like is not known.
(BMIHT/Rover)

follow, the latter powered by an in-line overhead-cam unit. Initially envisaged as a 1-litre, but soon upgraded to 1100cc, this was part of a family of ohc engines being developed by Morris: it would have been a smaller sister to the 1476cc Wolseley 4/50 unit and the 2215cc 'six' used in the Wolseley 6/80 and the Morris Six.

Nuffield Organisation management at this time was clearly in a state of some confusion, not helped by the eccentric interventions of Lord Nuffield, who in common with other members of the Morris board saw no need to replace the well-selling Eight, for which there was a hefty waiting list. Under pressure from his lordship, it was decided in 1946 to keep the Morris Eight Series E in production, postpone the Mosquito for a few months, and at first launch the new car solely as a Wolseley. The 'Wolseley Wasp' would be launched in September 1947 and the Morris, in two-door and four-door form, in January 1948.

. . . and nearly launched as an MG

The 'Wolseley first' plan was then briefly reversed, before management adopted *another* scheme in the spring of 1947. With costings for the Issigonis design looking worryingly high, and Lord Nuffield still negative about the car, the new Big Idea was to ditch the Mosquito, and launch the model, still in January 1948, as an up-market MG, powered by the ohc engine. The 'MG 1100' would be built in small numbers at Cowley, but driven to MG's Abingdon works for final checking, to bolster the fiction that it was an MG. Meanwhile the Morris Eight would continue, in a facelifted form, and at some stage in the future the Wasp would join the Nuffield range.

This scheme was confirmed two months later, in June 1947, at which time the MG's proposed launch slipped to March 1948 and the 'Wolseley Wasp' was cancelled. The reason given by Miles Thomas was that with a flat-rate

An ungainly tombstone grille characterises this 'MG 1100' try-out of 1947; the car was in fact envisaged as being a two-door.
(BMIHT/Rover)

road tax of £10, bigger-capacity cars would be favoured, and higher-priced small cars such as the Wasp would not be popular 'unless their performance offered outstanding attraction'. At the same time, as related in Chapter Three, the flat-four engine was abandoned.

A 1947 photo showing a prototype Mosquito with MG-style octagonal instrument surrounds can safely be assumed to be a representation of how an MG-badged Mosquito might have been presented. Interestingly, the talk was of the 'MG 1100' being a two-door, yet photos of mock-ups show only four-door cars.

But even the idea of an MG-badged Mosquito was abandoned, during the energy crisis of autumn 1947. With the government encouraging the idea of car manufacturers limiting the number of different models made, in September 1947 Lord Nuffield helped persuade the board to put the 'MG 1100' on ice and instead concentrate efforts on the bigger Oxford.

A bigger side-valve engine

By October 1947 sanity had started to prevail, under considerable pressure from a clearly exasperated Sir Miles Thomas, then Nuffield vice-chairman but shortly to be elbowed out. Talk of warming over the Series E with a facelift and independent front suspension was abandoned: it had been calculated that this folly would have cost more than the Mosquito. Instead, a mass-production Morris-badged model would be introduced at the 1948 Motor Show. The proposed MG and Wolseley versions were put back on the shelf — unsurprisingly, perhaps, given that the Wasp engine and gearbox package was going to cost almost twice as much to make as the Morris Eight engine and gearbox. Finally, maybe as a sop to Lord Nuffield, there was talk of keeping the Eight going until March 1949.

With the flat-four canned, the only remaining twists to the story concern the car's power unit. Two possibilities

This second 1947 proposal for the MG is slightly more harmonious. (BMIHT/Rover)

were briefly on the table: either a side-valve version of the ultimately still-born 1100cc Wolseley ohc engine, or a bored-out 950cc or 980cc version of the Eight's unit. Logic ultimately dictated, however, that using the 918cc side-valve unchanged was the best solution, and it was with this engine that the Mosquito, renamed the Minor, was finally launched in October 1948.

A Minor cabriolet?

No – not a drophead. Or a tourer. We're talking a soft-top in the French and German pre-war style, with solid side-rails and a simple fold-back hood. Fanciful? Well, a 1946 Cowley mock-up for a Wolseley version of the Mosquito not only features the longer wheelbase of the proposed Wolseley and MG variants, but also has a convertible top.

Look carefully at the photo and you'll see a fabric top running from the top of the windscreen to the back of the car. Look inside the car and the rear

window is clearly smaller than the regular screen. An interesting idea – but there's no evidence that a car to this configuration was ever built. During 1946 there was, however, talk of a 'folding-top Mosquito', which it can be assumed refers to this type of body rather than to a fully-open tourer. A July 1946 planning chart even talks of either a two-door or a four-door cabriolet, although how serious this was is not clear. In any case, response to the idea of any sort of cabriolet was lukewarm.

'With regard to the Cabriolet, there did not seem to be any insistent demand for this sort of body either from the Export or the Home market,' Sir Miles Thomas says in a February 1946 memo. 'Indeed, opinion seemed to be that the ultimate option of a sliding roof . . . would be preferable.'

A Minor-based MG sports car?

Here there's an element of supposition involved. Photographic evidence shows

This 1946 photo shows what is thought to be the first Wolseley Wasp mock-up – but note the 'convertible-saloon' fabric roof with its smaller rear screen. The radiator seems a size too big, and extends well below the bumper. The extra metal between the front wheelarch and the door is evidence of the longer wheelbase intended for the Wolseley/MG versions of the Mosquito. (BMIHT/Rover)

that in the 1946–48 period Cowley was looking at a new slab-sided MG sports car. This was coded 'DO926' and had strong Mosquito/Minor motifs in its styling. This is no surprise, given that the Issigonis sketchbooks of this time include drawings of an MG sports car — including a sketch of a car with a retractable metal roof. The new MG was intended to use the overhead-cam 1100cc engine mooted for the still-born 'MG 1100' and Wolseley Wasp, and it seems reasonable to assume that the chassis would have been based on Minor components.

It is generally believed that the car, referred to as the 'Midget Major', never proceeded beyond mock-up stage. However, Sir Miles Thomas wrote in November 1947 to Vic Oak and Alec Issigonis that he would 'like it determined whether we can fit a $1\frac{1}{2}$-litre OHC engine in the new Midget'. He goes on to say how he was aware that the car 'was originally designed for an 1100cc unit'. This rather suggests that design work had proceeded further

than the mere creation of a styling mock-up.

The notion of an MG built around Minor mechanicals resurfaced in the mid-'50s, when Abingdon — having regained its design autonomy — was asked by BMC management to look at how a cheap sports car could be constructed around the Minor floorpan. An MG experimental number, EX 188, was allocated to the project, but it seems that the idea was not pursued. Healey, meanwhile, was working on what became the Austin-Healey Sprite, and once this had been approved by BMC there was no incentive to push on with EX188.

The Minor 'People's Car'

At the time of the Korean War there was considerable fear that a full-scale national emergency would develop. Against this background, and with steel already scarce, the Morris directors discussed an 'austerity' Minor, as board minutes for 1 February 1951 reveal:

The mock-up for an MG Midget, presumed to be based on the Mosquito/Minor, nestles between an MG YT tourer and a Minor MM in this line-up of the proposed 1949 Nuffield range. The car was also photographed fitted with a hard-top. (BMIHT/Rover)

'The Vice-Chairman suggested that the Organisation should be in a position to offer a "People's Car" in the event of a national emergency. It was decided to prepare a Morris Minor, painted War Office green and stripped of all embellishments, and hold it in reserve as an example of what could be offered.'

It is not certain whether such a Minor was ever built. However, the project was formally cancelled at the 20 June 1951 board meeting.

Coachbuilt Minors

At the same 1 February 1951 board meeting as the 'People's Car' was discussed, vice-chairman Reginald Hanks also broached the possibility of offering 'full-chassis' versions of the Minor and the Oxford, for bodying by outside coachbuilders:

If the 1951 proposal to sell the Minor and Oxford in 'full-chassis' form had come to fruition, we could well have seen coachbuilt variants similar to this Cunard Utility Car based on the 10cwt Morris Cowley chassis/cab unit. (Richard Cownden)

'The Vice-Chairman suggested that the effect of the steel shortage might be lessened if the Organisation were to produce full-chassis editions of the Morris Minor and the Morris Oxford on which various types of passenger and commercial bodies, either wooden or steel, might be mounted abroad, or even at home. Mr Oak undertook to produce sample chassis.'

Given that the chassised Minor and Cowley van and pick-up models were well advanced by this stage, such a notion was certainly feasible. Indeed, the odd coachbuilder would in the future offer a 'woody' estate on both Minor and Cowley LCV (light commercial vehicle) chassis.

The idea was still under consideration in early May 1951, when the board was awaiting feedback from the Sales Department before formulating a production programme. By the end of the month, however, the concept had been abandoned. If sheet steel were the only scarce material, the project might be viable. But if other materials became scarce, it was argued, there would be no benefit in encouraging a switch to coachbuilt construction using wood and aluminium. Adding supplementary models to the range would also exacerbate the serious problems already existing with the supply of spare parts.

The 'Lady's Minor'

Back in 1951 or thereabouts, according to former Morris engineer Jim Lambert, the Nuffield Experimental Department created what they called the 'Lady's Minor'. A two-door 'low-light' with polychromatic pale green paintwork, it had two-tone green fabric upholstery and a central speedometer – this last pre-dating the later Series II arrangement by some years. An interesting detail was that the seat backs incorporated a chrome rail so they could be moved back and forth without marking the upholstery. This very pre-war type of seat had earlier been seen on various Mosquito prototypes.

The Wolseley-engined Minors

More fundamentally different were the Minors fitted in 1951/52 with the overhead-valve 918cc Wolseley Eight engine – simply a pushrod derivative of the Series E unit. The Minor almost reached production in this form.

'It was superb – it was a beautiful engine, which really made the Minor,' recalls Jack Daniels. Instead, the Minor was lumbered with the weedy 803cc Austin A30 engine.

'The Austin engine in this form was hopeless – the things needed a new crankshaft every 20,000 miles,' remembers Jim Lambert. 'You just compare the size of the journals with those on the old Morris Eight engine. We had a super engine, a super gearbox, and a good strong back axle. We were very disappointed to be forced into using Austin units instead – it was a real step backwards.'

The full story behind why the Morris Minor never got this engine is told in Chapter Five.

Moulton rubber suspension

Other experimental Minors of this pre-BMC period included one with Moulton rubber springing. 'We ran it on the pavé at MIRA for 1,000 miles, and it gave no trouble. It was significant in that it confirmed that rubber was a serious medium for car springing,' says Alex Moulton.

To pass a 1,000-mile pavé test was a key requirement for all Nuffield models, but all the same Daniels wasn't particularly impressed by the Moulton-suspended Minor: the main aim of the exercise for him had been to see if the new suspension would reduce road noise – which it didn't.

The front-wheel-drive Minor

Perhaps the most famous one-off of the period was the transverse-engined front-wheel-drive Minor described by Jack Daniels in Chapter Two. The car is still fondly remembered by fellow Nuffield Organisation engineers, in particular for its superb roadholding in treacherous weather. 'You could really dice with it on ice,' says former BMC

'Morris-Healey' is spurned by Nuffield

A Healey-Minor? No thanks. In May 1949 Nuffield vice-chairman Reginald Hanks had talks with Donald Healey. Then making cars powered by the Riley 2½-litre engine, Healey wanted to be supplied with Morris Minor panels. This may well have been in connection with a project cooked up between Issigonis and the Healey company for the production of a 'super-sports' Minor fitted with the big Riley twin-cam engine. Nothing came of the meeting – in fact Nuffield wanted as little as possible to do with Healey and his schemes.

Director of Engineering Charles Griffin, then a Morris experimental engineer.

Equally impressed was Gerald Palmer, the Chief Designer for MG, Wolseley and Riley who in 1952 became Chief Engineer for all Nuffield cars. 'Jack Daniels, two others and myself tried out the fwd Minor against a standard Minor on the hill from Watlington on a snowy, bitter winter's day. Whereas the rear-drive car could only get halfway up and would then slither off the road, the front-wheel-drive Minor would chug on and on up to the top. It was quite a convincing demonstration.'

'It was absolutely fantastic,' confirms Jim Lambert. 'The steering was awful, with it tugging away like a *Traction Avant* Citroën's, but its actual steerability was terrific, and in bad conditions its roadholding was fantastic. I loved it, and reckon it was the best Minor ever.'

The Issigonis 'New Minor'

Meanwhile, though, thoughts on a

rebodied Minor weren't long in coming. The earliest proposals seem to have been some quarter-scale models presented in 1951. Stark, glassy and slab-sided, they have much of the Series II Oxford about them. By 1953 there was a full-scale mock-up with one side as a four-door and the other as a two-door; evoking even more strongly the next-generation Oxford, it looked not unpleasing.

The Palmer 'New Minor'

By this stage, however, Issigonis had left to work at Alvis, and his characteristically austere proposals began to be given more form, under the direction of Gerald Palmer – the man responsible for the Magnette ZA and Wolseley 4/44 and the bigger Riley Pathfinder and Wolseley 6/90 duo.

Alas, the simple, honest old Morris

This quarter-scale model dated 1951 shows the original idea for a restyled Minor. Very reminiscent of the Series II Oxford, it clearly shows the hand of Issigonis, not least in the Mini-like grille. Another photo shows a wider and less tall variation on the same type of grille. (BMIHT/Rover)

The same basic design in full-sized 1953 mock-up form is here presented as a four-door on one side and a two-door on the other. The car now looks even more like the Series II Oxford launched in 1954. (BMIHT/Rover)

Minor seemed to be losing its way: some of the suggestions were pretty odd, to say the least. First the car's harmonious but rather bland lines were developed to incorporate a traditional vertical radiator shell, and the slab sides given a little more form. Then – under the aegis of Palmer – a full restyle was initiated. Surviving photos show an ungainly saloon, in two-door and four-door formats, with a panoramic front screen and a somewhat contrived grille treatment.

Today Palmer denies any personal responsibility for this design, although he does say that about this time he did come up with a proposal for a panoramic-screened Minor replacement, and that a mock-up was built. Given the italianate elegance of Palmer's Magnette and the similarly harmonious forms of the Riley Pathfinder and its

Still dated 1953, this mock-up attempts to give the 'New Minor' more form. Lord Nuffield would have approved of the pre-war style of upright grille. (BMIHT/Rover)

This fresh proposal from 1954 was created when Gerald Palmer was in charge of Morris design, but today he denies any responsibility for this car. Again the mock-up is a two-door on one side and a four-door on the other. (BMIHT/Rover)

The near side of the same DO 1058 'New Minor' emphasises the proposal's lacklustre lines. (BMIHT/Rover)

Meanwhile Dick Burzi's styling studio at Longbridge was feeling its way towards a 'New Minor' of its own. This dumpy design seems to have been influenced by Ford's 100E Anglia and Prefect. (BMIHT/Rover)

Wolseley sister, it is indeed hard to believe that a man with such a sure touch could have come up with something so clumsy.

Whether there was one wraparound-screen 'New Minor' proposal or two, one thing is certain: BMC management championed a restyle by long-time Austin stylist Dick Burzi. Palmer remembers the episode with some sadness:

'I forget whether it was Leonard Lord or his deputy, George Harriman, but they came in one day and tossed a picture on my desk, saying, "This is the new body styling for the next Minor, done by Burzi." Any work I had been doing was ignored, and Burzi was given the job independently, behind my back. I suppose it was fair enough, to get two minds working on the same problem . . .'

But Palmer clearly wasn't pleased at such boorish management practices, and differences of opinion led to his leaving Nuffield in late 1955 to join Vauxhall.

Thoughts return to a Wolseley-Minor

The idea of a Wolseley-badged Minor seems not to have gone away, judging by a £50,000 capital allocation in January 1954 for tooling for a 'Wolseley 8hp four-door saloon'. It would appear from this that a Wolseley derivative of the 'New Minor' was under consideration. Ultimately, as told below, the 'New Minor' didn't happen, but one of the cars spawned by the project was indeed a small Minor-derived Wolseley. This was the 1500, a vehicle that had an engine considerably bigger than the 948cc A-series unit that any '8hp' model would surely have ended up using.

The Minor that became a Major

After one or two horrors, Burzi eventually came up with a conservative if slightly fussy proposal for the 'New Minor', which was now to be powered by the 1200cc version of the BMC B-series engine. But by this time – around the end of 1955 – work was well in hand on the 948cc A-series power unit. Additionally, Issigonis was back in the BMC fold and would inevitably be turning his thoughts to a new Minor of his own – front-wheel-drive in all likelihood.

Re-tooling for a new conventionally engineered Minor thus began to look questionable; with some styling re-touches and the much-improved bigger A-series engine, the original Minor could happily continue in production until Issigonis came up with an all-new replacement. This is what happened, and sales of the 1956-introduced Minor 1000 proved the wisdom of this decision.

As for Burzi's 'New Minor', this was moved up-market, and launched in April 1957 as the Wolseley 1500, followed in November by the Riley One-Point-Five. It was a close-run thing, though: right into 1957 the original stripped-out Morris version was a production possibility, in both two-door and four-door format, with the designation Morris 1200. There were also at least three different estate car proposals, again both two-door and four-door.

That wasn't the end of the story, however. The original Morris version wasn't put away, but instead was sent to Australia, where it surfaced in 1958 as the 1489cc Morris Major and Austin Lancer. The full saga of the Major is told in Chapter Six.

Strut suspension for the Minor

Following Ford's introduction of strut suspension in Britain, with the 1950 Consul and Zephyr, various manufacturers looked at the use of struts – including Rover, whose engineers were not impressed. Jack Daniels recalls a strut front suspension being tried on the Minor, and photos suggest that this was in 1956. The experiment was quickly abandoned, as the roll-free handling made the cars dangerous, in his opinion.

Improving the Minor

By this time the Minor was clearly going to be around for some years to

Longbridge also looked at ways of updating the existing Minor. This 1953 model shows a revised waistline moulding, swages on both front and rear wings, a front wing extended further into the doors, and a fresh grille and headlamp treatment. (Rover/author's collection)

come. To keep it up-to-date, revised rear suspension was felt vital. Softer rear springs were one option, discussed by Issigonis in a 1957 BMC memo that also suggested an improved dashboard and the introduction of duo-tone colour schemes.

Independent rear suspension

Thoughts soon moved on to an independent rear, envisaged as using trailing arms and coil springs. This was referred to in a 1957 memo from Technical Director S. V. Smith to Charles Griffin:

'We discussed with the Chairman . . . the possibility of extending the life of the Morris Minor by the introduction of independent rear springing.

'When this modification is brought through – which must be given priority – you will introduce, at the same time, the new facia . . . and also a modifica-

tion to the grille. This grille, I suggest, should take the form of the existing surround, and in place of the bars I think we could use the present Isis mesh.'

The irs was built into a Minor, as recounted by Jack Daniels in Chapter Two. Coil springs were, however, to the best of his recollection never tried. 'I don't discount it as a possibility, but it doesn't tie in with the set-up I remember. The trouble with coils is that you'd have to push them up into the wheelarch, and that would narrow the boot-space just where you wouldn't want it narrowed.'

Charles Griffin is equally definite that coils were never in the picture. Certainly it was in the form using a laminated square-section torsion bar that Jim Lambert tested the independent-rear Minor. His recollections are less rosy than those of Daniels, although his trial of the car may have been at an

This 1958 proposal for a smarter-looking dashboard 'de-humps' the instrument panel and introduces a padded top rail. Somewhat inconveniently, a radio lurks behind the driver's glovebox lid, which only opens part-way. (BMIHT/Rover)

early stage in its development before the angle of inclination for the arms had been optimised.

'It was awful,' he says. 'It was all over the place – the car handled like a pig. You didn't know whether it was going to understeer or oversteer. The handling wasn't improved, and the ride wasn't any better.'

In the end the system was offered to BMC in Australia, for introduction on the Series II Major and Lancer, but was vetoed by the Australians on grounds of its extra cost.

And the 'Isis' grille and revised dashboard? A restyled dashboard was photographed in 1958. It featured a padded and de-humped top rail incorporating an ashtray, and a somewhat awkward radio installation in the driver's side glovebox; it never reached production. As for the Isis-style grille mesh, this was tried on the Minor, as another 1958 Cowley photo testifies. What's

interesting is that in the photo there appears to be an archaic gilled-tube radiator lurking behind the grille. That really is a puzzle . . .

The Hydrolastic Minor

Still on suspension, in a rather different league was the Minor used as a development car in 1956/57, at the time when Issigonis was working with Alex Moulton on rubber-and-fluid suspension systems. This 'mule' – still rear-wheel-drive – had softly mounted subframes front and rear, and used an embryonic form of Hydrolastic as already tried in XC9001.

The interconnected suspension system was at a fairly early stage in its development, and initially used long-stroke hydraulic displacers at each wheel, connected front to rear by a full-length rubber sausage running the length of either side of the car and filled with

Rather old-fashioned in feel, this alternative proposal for a new Traveller retains the existing curved window frames.
(BMIHT/Rover)

fluid. This sausage had spline-like outer serrations and was restrained by a braided sheath. In use it twitched around somewhat disconcertingly, and it also had a tendency to puncture. 'It was called the Python because it seemed to be alive,' recalls Alex Moulton. 'When it was being driven down to Issigonis and myself in Monte Carlo, it had to be tamed by being wired up with wire from a wine cask. It gave a very, very floaty ride, but it was wonderfully flat and comfortable.'

Subsequently fluid-filled rubber 'cheeses' – cylindrical rubber units with fluid reservoirs – were used in place of the Python, one 'cheese' being positioned centrally on each side of the car, with hard interconnection pipes running front to rear.

An all-steel Traveller

Meanwhile, final thoughts on updating the Minor's bodywork continued, with the emphasis on a new estate version with all-steel bodywork. In 1956 two proposals were presented, both with four doors. One had a curved back and retained the saloon's rear doors in their entirety, while the other had squarer lines and revised framing for the doors.

All change becomes no change

By this stage, though, the best policy for the Minor was to leave it largely alone: work was steaming ahead on what ultimately became the 1100, and the Minor was looking very much like yesterday's technology. Before the Suez crisis sidelined the 1100 in favour of the Mini, the likelihood was that the Minor would be replaced by 1960 – or not much later. And so Issigonis's friendly little 'Poached Egg' carried on unchanged . . .

Chapter Five

The Wolseley-engined Minor

TALK TO FORMER Morris engineers about the Minor, and as the conversation drifts round to power units you can be sure that sooner or later the subject of the Wolseley Eight engine will come up. The story is always the same: it was a lovely engine, it came close to being installed in the Minor, and it would have transformed the car. So what's all the fuss about,

and why didn't the Minor get the overhead-valve Wolseley unit?

Wolseley's new baby

The Wolseley Eight was supposed to be launched in autumn 1939 as a new model for the 1940 model year, and as a follow-on to the Morris Eight Series E introduced at the 1938 Motor Show.

The Wolseley Eight (foreground) was only made in small numbers; it was an upmarket version of the Morris Eight Series E seen behind. (Tony Baker/Classic & Sports Car)

Alas, the outbreak of war prevented the Wolseley's introduction, and it was not until March 1946 that it was formally announced. However, on the very day that war was declared *The Autocar* was engaged on a 1,400-mile road test of the prototype, and in its 29 September 1939 issue the weekly magazine was able to report on what it termed 'a remarkable new small car'.

In fact the Wolseley wasn't all that new. It was essentially an up-market version of the Morris Eight, sharing the same basic body but having traditional Wolseley frontal styling and such detail enhancements as the fitment of running boards. Inside it was more luxurious, of course, with a wooden dashboard and many subtle improvements. The real novelty, however, was under the

bonnet. In place of the Series E's side-valve engine – called the 'USHM' – was an overhead-valve adaptation of the Morris unit, delivering 33bhp in place of the E's 29.5bhp. Although not mentioned by *The Autocar* in its description of the car in March 1946, there was one unusual feature to the Wolseley's 'UPHW' engine: in place of an ortho-dox timing chain, the camshaft was driven by a 'Fabroil' fibre-reinforced-plastic gear off a steel pinion on the nose of the crankshaft. The reason for this would appear to have been to achieve greater quietness.

The use of direct gear drive seems to have been a late decision. Certainly in March 1943 Engines Branch works manager Jack Shaw told Sir Miles Thomas that the ohv engines in the pro-

The Wolseley Eight UPHW engine and its matching gearbox, as shared with the Morris Eight. (BMIHT/Rover)

totype Wolseley Eights used by Lord Nuffield and another director had been removed, overhauled, and fitted with a gear-driven camshaft in place of the chain drive used until then.

The Eight on test

After journeying from London to the Highlands and back, and recording an overall 39mpg, *The Autocar* was definitely won over by the little Wolseley — and by its power unit.

'The ohv engine is smooth and produces really useful acceleration, not only if the gears are used from the lower speeds but also in top gear from surprisingly high speeds,' reported the magazine. 'A definite surge forward can be felt from an indicated 50mph when the throttle pedal is put hard down, and the pleasant running at a speedometer 60 is outstandingly good, making it necessary to remind yourself that you are in a car rated at only 8hp . . .'

A life cut short

The Wolseley was indeed an appealing package — as Lord Nuffield himself acknowledged, by running the 1939 prototype tested by *The Autocar* as his personal transport until 1955. The advertising copywriters certainly weren't shy in highlighting the niche occupied by the Eight. 'This post-war car creates its own class since it transcends all conventional conceptions of the 8hp car,' ran a May 1946 advert.

Alas, thanks to its late start, production of the Wolseley Eight was relatively shortlived. Manufacture only began in March 1946, and the last example left the lines in October 1948. In all a mere 5,344 were made, against 120,434 Morris Eight Series Es.

Why the Minor needed a new engine

Once all the pre-production sagas concerning the Mosquito/Minor had been played out, it was with the old Morris Eight side-valve engine that the car was launched. This was a pragmatic decision in terms of the production processes, since it avoided any dislocation at Morris Engines Branch. It also gave the Minor a tested and reliable power unit.

However, it was soon clear that the little flathead, now rated at 27.5bhp, was barely up to the task. It gave the two-door Minor an adequate if thoroughly unsparkling performance, but its work was cut out trying to power the half-hundredweight-heavier four-door. Worse, tests of the prototype Minor van proved that performance — presumably when ballasted to the proposed 5cwt payload — was lamentable. This was a serious blow: the van was intended to account for over 20 per cent of Minor output.

Minutes from the Morris Motors directors' meeting of 2 August 1950 emphasise the gravity of the situation:

'Mr Oak reported that tests of the proposed new 5cwt van had revealed a totally unacceptable performance. After discussion, it was agreed that unless very much better results could be obtained . . . the new project would be abandoned, and production of the existing 5cwt van [ie the Eight-derived Series Z] might continue indefinitely.'

Enter the Wolseley engine

By the 29 November 1950 board meeting a clear decision had been made:

New to 'U'?

A word of explanation about Nuffield engine codes. 'U' was the series of engine, 'S' stood for side-valve, 'H' for the eighth letter of the alphabet and thus for 8hp, and 'M' for the marque — ie Morris. Hence 'USHM' means a side-valve U-series 8hp Morris engine. The Wolseley Eight engine was a 'UPHW' — U-series, pushrod, 8hp, and Wolseley. Had it entered production in the Minor it would thus have become a 'UPHM'.

'It was resolved as a matter of future policy that overhead valves should be incorporated in the Morris Minor engine. It would not be possible for the changeover to be immediate, and it would therefore be spread over a period, the start of which would be dependent on the availability of new machine tools recently authorised for Engines Branch.'

This scheme for a phased introduction of the Wolseley ohv engine was clarified at the 13 December 1950 board meeting:

'Mr Oak reported he had driven a car equipped with a prototype engine which had shown excellent promise. It was anticipated that it would be possible for full-scale production to begin early in 1952, which would mean that the present Morris Minor would continue in its present basic form for a little over a year.

'A limited number of engines, amounting to some 300 a week, could be ready towards the end of 1951 and, if deemed advisable, would be available for incorporation in four-door models or in vans, for which the ohv engine would provide the improved performance required.'

Clearly, then, it was regarded as relatively pressing that the ohv engine be available in the four-door and van: sufficiently pressing, the implication is, for production to begin using the existing low-volume tooling left over from Wolseley Eight days.

This would be a temporary measure, until new machines could be installed. In July 1951 this was actioned, board minutes for 25 July noting capital authorisation to a value of £99,942 in respect of '106 machine tools required for production of 8hp ohv engine at rate of 2,100 per week'. That was serious business: at the end of 1950 Morris Engines was gunning for a weekly output of 4,915 engines, of which

2,300 would be 8hp units. The capital authorisation thus meant only one thing. The Wolseley engine would become the mainstream 8hp unit for the Nuffield Organisation, with output of the side-valve unit being restricted to military and marine use.

The programme falters

Alas, signs of slippage in the programme were already apparent. Vic Oak continued to envisage the ohv engine being introduced first in the four-door and later in the two-door, and the idea of a 1951 Motor Show launch for the ohv four-door was clearly in his mind.

George Dono, general manager of Nuffield Metal Products, pointed out at the 25 July 1951 board meeting that this was now looking unrealistic:

'Mr Dono mentioned that all the necessary modifications to the body had not yet been notified to Nuffield Metal Products. These would take some time to finalise, although they seemed likely to be of a minor nature. It was regarded as impossible for the four-door Minor with ohv engine to be ready for exhibition at the 1951 Show.'

Although it may not have been apparent, the project was now starting to slip away. Certainly there was a tinge of crisis in the air by autumn 1951 — by which time, remember, it had been hoped to announce the ohv-powered four-door Minor. This prompted a special Morris Motors directors' meeting on 3 October 1951, devoted specifically to the ohv engine as a result of 'particulars of production expectations which had proved to be inaccurate'. The chief of Morris Engines Branch, 'Nobby' Clark, laid the whole sorry story on the table:

'In the course of full discussion Mr Clark explained that the major issue controlling the production of Morris Minor ohv engines was the availability of the Cylinder Block Transfer Machine, which had been prejudiced by the following circumstances:

(a) When the acquisition of the machines originated, the Board had been thinking in terms of a larger side-valve engine.
(b) When it was decided to introduce an ohv engine, certain complications inevitably arose, and much of the design work already devoted to the Transfer Machine had perforce to be modified.
(c) The effect of re-armament upon the Machine Tool industry has resulted in a general postponement of delivery dates.
(d) The handicap created by the necessity to adopt SAE threads.
(e) The foregoing delays had resulted in Austin's placing an order with Archdale's for a Transfer Machine.

'It was hoped that the Transfer Machine would be in full operation by January 1953.

'It was established that deliveries of Morris Minor ohv engines could start at 50 per week in February 1952, rising to 300 per week by April or May 1952. This would result in a corresponding reduction in the production of SV engines, which would fall from 1,400 to 1,100 per week approximately. It was decided, however, that it would not be expedient to announce the ohv engine until considerably later in the year.

'Endeavour would be made to build up a stock of ohv engines at an appropriate time, which would cater for initial CKD requirements, enable Morris Minor four-door ohv car production to commence at the 1952 Motor Show, and thereafter to be maintained at not less than 500 units per week.'

Too late the hero . . .

A year had been lost, in effect — to a large degree as a result of the Korean War, but also as a consequence of internal delays. Clearly, at some stage the idea of the 980cc bored-out side-valve engine had re-entered the picture, and Morris had also set out to remove the anomaly of metric threads in the engine, a feature dating back to the days of the Bullnose's Hotchkiss-derived engine.

The best that could be hoped for, in such circumstances, was a phased introduction of the ohv engine, beginning with the debut of a re-engined four-door at the 1952 Motor Show. The launch of the rival Austin A30 at the 1951 Show wasn't seen as changing anything, as board minutes dated 30 October 1951 indicate. However, the arrival of the Austin did emphasise the importance of getting the ohv engine on stream:

'It was agreed that in spite of the advent of the new Austin Seven, no anxiety need be entertained regarding the future of the Morris Minor, which was considered to possess at least another four years of useful life. It was thought to be of the first importance to do everything possible to expedite the introduction of the ohv engine, and to ensure that the prices of the Morris Minor models continue to be competitive.'

Little did the Nuffield directors know that a month later they would be discussing the proposed – and duly ratified – merger of the Nuffield Organisation with the Austin Motor Company Ltd. All references to the ohv engine in Morris board minutes cease at this point; in July 1952 the export four-door Minor was given the Austin A30's 803cc pushrod engine. The Minor had got its ohv engine, and comfortably ahead of Morris's planned launch of its re-engined car. It wasn't the right engine, it wasn't a halfway good engine, but the Nuffield team had been comprehensively out-smarted by ruthless Austin boss Leonard Lord. But was skullduggery involved?

Dirty work at Longbridge?

'We got to the stage where tooling had been ordered from America to increase production capacity for the Wolseley engine – and I believe the tools were actually on the ships and coming over when the BMC merger happened and the plan was abandoned. We got that near to it!'

Such were the recollections of Jack Daniels, when the author first interviewed him back in 1988. Reflecting today on the question, Daniels now feels reasonably confident that the tooling arrived in Britain as scheduled.

'The story I have is that the machinery was diverted to the Longbridge side where it promptly disappeared. Although I can't vouch for that, because I never saw it, it is said to have arrived in England, and said to have been dispatched to the Austin side, instead of the Morris side, and to have disappeared forthwith. Certainly Bill Appleby of Austin's Engine Division wouldn't have had tooling for any other engine lying about . . .'

John Barker, who was an engineer in the Morris Engines Branch Experimental Department at the time, is able to confirm that the machinery did in fact arrive at the Morris engine plant at Courthouse Green.

'We'd reached the stage of getting the transfer machines ready for it to go into production. We were a long, long way down the road – imagine the amount of space all the machines took up on the factory floor and the planning that would have to have gone on to install them.

'Sid Barron, the Chief Planning Engineer, was assured the engine was going into production, and then overnight "The Austin" had its way, and the A30 engine took over. He was very, very bitter. He had done so much

work to get the Wolseley engine into production. He was terribly upset, and really felt very let down.'

The elimination of the Wolseley engine was a hurtful blow to Nuffield engineers, who without exception are today scathing about the original 803cc version of the A-series engine. It also had a serious short-term impact on Morris Engines Branch, which lost the centre of gravity of its manufacturing programme when the Austin-produced A-series supplanted the side-valve Morris unit.

In terms of the economies of mass-production, the decision had strong merits. Austin had tooled up for extensive production of a modern pushrod engine, while Morris was lagging on its tooling-up, and this for an engine that was essentially an adapted pre-war unit. In the end the A-series came good, and the Minor thrived with its Austin motorisation. But there was a four-year black hole from 1952 until 1956, during which the Morris was powered by a weak, poorly geared engine that did it no favours. Accidents of timing and the imperatives of industrial politics had deprived the Minor of the power unit it so badly needed.

'A beautiful engine' . . .

Was the Wolseley engine really worth the tears cried over it? 'It was superb – it was a beautiful engine which really made the Minor,' recalls Jack Daniels. 'I drove the prototype Wolseley-engined Minor a lot – probably more than anybody. Once I borrowed it for a holiday in the West Country, and I had the best ride across Bodmin Moor that I've ever had. I loved it. It went very well – the traffic was nose-to-tail and I took everything in sight. There was nothing to stop me. It was a really nice little car, with a good performance. I'm still of the opinion that had we been able to put the 918cc ohv engine in the Minor that would have been magnificent.'

Former Nuffield engineer Jim Lambert seconds this judgement. 'We were absolutely stunned when they said the engine had to be thrown out. It was a beautiful smooth engine, and much better than the A30 unit. It was better than satisfactory – we were over the moon with it. Not only that, but it was married to a good axle. With the A30 engine you hadn't gone far down the road before the big ends dropped out . . .'

. . . or a liability ?

Those who have run aged Wolseley Eights in the 1950s and '60s are not always so eulogistic. The 'Fabroil' timing gear – also found on Morris 'MO' Oxfords – is a known Achilles Heel, disintegrating with potentially disastrous results. Supplies of new gears were not long in drying up, with the result that cars were often re-engined with side-valve Morris Eight units. Attempts of late to remanufacture the gears in Tufnol or in nylon have not been successful, and the only answer these days is to have a gear wheel expensively machined from oiled steel or phosphor-bronze. If properly cut

The Wolseley engine exploded – a very different beast from the Morris side-valve. (Wolseley Motors)

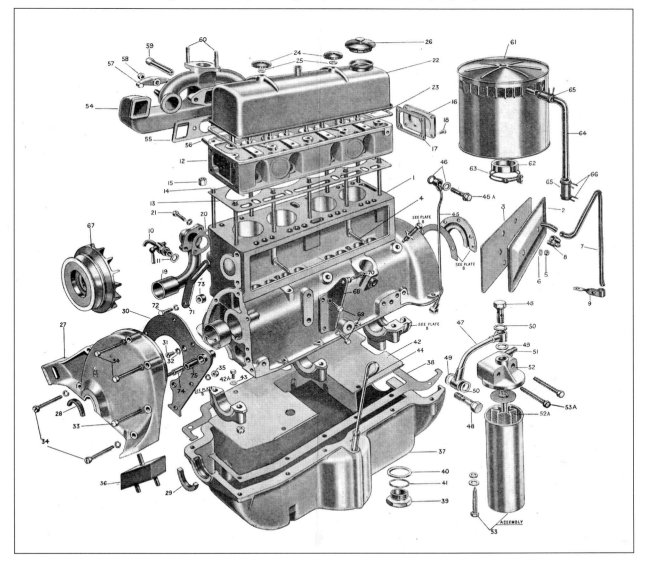

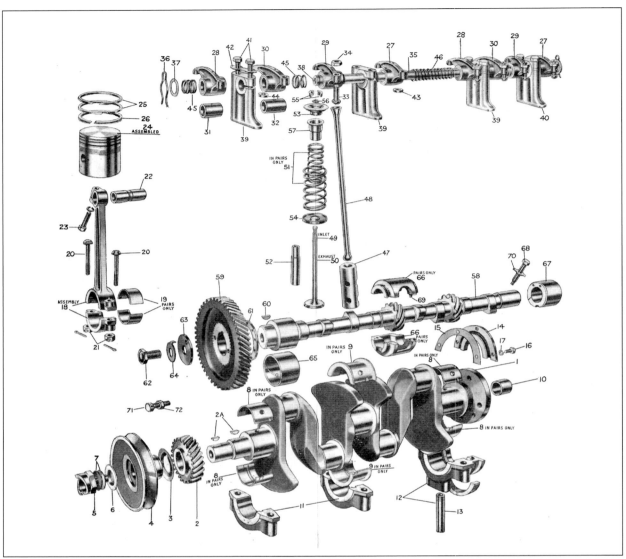

these should last well, but the pay-off is additional noise – to the point where at tickover the car can sound like a diesel. Another problem, apparently, is that the engine is supposedly prone to blowing its head gasket.

'The engine was an under-developed disaster. In the 15 years I owned it, the car was a bag of mechanical trouble – all engine-related,' says one disillusioned former owner. 'The Wolseley Eight was a beautiful museum piece but not a practical car.'

Put such remarks to one-time Nuffield engineers and they are per-plexed. 'I never had timing gear problems,' says Jack Daniels. 'I don't recall it being regarded as unreliable and I wasn't aware of any abnormal problems. The engine was a known quantity and there wasn't much discussion about putting it in the Minor – it was a natural choice. The decision to use it was almost automatic.'

Tony Jennings, a former engineer at Morris Engines Branch, supports this view. 'There were no reliability problems of which I was aware. As a power unit the A-series wasn't in the same league.'

The reciprocating components and pushrod mechanism of the Wolseley engine – note (No 59) the 'Fabroil' timing gear. (Wolseley Motors)

The Wolseley engine

In an ideal world one would find a Wolseley Eight engine, install it in a Minor, and report on what one found. With precious few spare UPHW engines kicking about, the next best solution is a back-to-back comparison of a Morris Eight Series E and a Wolseley Eight, as the cars are essentially identical but for their engines. Thanks to the kindness of owners Martin Wills and Dave Bates, the author was recently able to do just this.

The side-valve engine in the Wills Series E is a contented and surprisingly smooth little workhorse, and on friendly terrain is capable of powering the Morris to an eventual maximum speed of 60mph. On a level road it will cruise happily at 45–50mph, and with a slope in your favour it pushes on to an indicated 55mph with impressive willingness.

But with the slope against you it's a different story. If you lose speed, you really lose it, and pulling up a hill without a downchange from top has the Morris nearly dying underneath you. In such circumstances you learn to change down in anticipation and keep the engine on the boil. In fairness, driving a low-powered 'modern' such as a 2CV or an 845cc Renault 4 in hilly terrain demands the same approach, but there's no doubting that the Series E has no great reserves of muscle.

The Wolseley of Dave Bates is a startling contrast. It feels instantly more responsive, revving freely and accelerating through the gears with a real brisk-ness. There's power to spare, whereas with the Morris you're always aware of the need to marshall the side-valve's limited resources with a degree of guile if you are not to run out of breath.

In the Wolseley a 50mph cruise is more than comfortable, and at an indicated 55mph the car is still accelerating; nor, as on the Morris, is one's foot flat to the floor. At this speed the engine does not feel strained, and indeed it is possible to take the Wolseley up to 60mph without feeling one is punishing the machinery. Hillclimbing is far less demanding, and the car will romp up inclines that would have you down-changing in the Morris.

Dave has fitted a phosphor-bronze timing wheel, and you can hear the 'tick-tick-tick' as it goes round. Under way, despite the dieselly tickover, it's not unpleasantly obtrusive: it merely takes an edge off what is otherwise a very sweet power unit. 'With the fibre timing wheel the car sounded so right — so quiet,' says Dave. 'The engine felt in character with the quality feel of the car. All you could hear was a little tappet noise.'

But even with the more metallic soundtrack of the car today, it's clear that the engine is a little gem, providing the spinsterish Wolseley with gratifying stamina. In feel the engine is not dissimilar to that of an Alta-converted side-valve, and there's no reason to doubt that a Minor fitted with the Wolseley power unit would not have had the same strong performance. No wonder so many people were upset when the engine was canned.

This 'highlight' MM catalogue is undated but would seem to be for the 1952 model year. The single sheet is twice folded to give the regular 11 x 8$\frac{1}{2}$ inch landscape format; colour is used throughout, with a mix of artwork and coloured mono photos.

The same cover image is used for three early Series II catalogues. From the top are: a Dutch-language catalogue dated 8/53 for the full Minor range; a dedicated 1952 catalogue for the four-door; and a British catalogue (dated 3/54) for the full Minor range. As the catalogue design was first seen in 1952, the Traveller was never included, but instead was given a separate catalogue.

The catalogue for the Series II Minor range (left) is dated 3/54, and borrows format, most illustrations, and layout and text from the 1952 MM catalogue featured earlier. The layout of the dedicated four-door catalogue (far left) of 9/52 rearranges some of the same basic artwork for its centre spread.

This small upright 'portrait format' eight-page Morris range catalogue is unstapled, and uses mono photos throughout, deeply sepia-tinted. It is undated, but as the Minor section features exclusively the Series II, but does not include the Traveller, the date would have to be early or mid-1953. On the cover it runs the 'You'll be glad you bought a Morris' slogan, but still uses the 'Quality First' slogan inside.

This small-format gilt-covered Morris range catalogue does not carry the Morris name or logo, merely the 'Quality First' slogan. It is undated, but the presence of the Minor 'Traveller's Car' – strangely not given any model title – identifies it as for the 1954 model year. The main artwork consists of monotone pastel sketches against a blue-grey background. No technical specifications are given – clearly this was a 'taster' catalogue.

The first catalogue for the Minor 'Traveller's Car' is shared with the Oxford version; the date is 10/53. The single 22 x 17 inch sheet folds twice to give the conventional 11 x 8½ inch landscape-format size. Inside is mainly colour artwork, but some coloured mono photos are used.

Two early US-market catalogues for the Minor 'Station Wagon': the mono single-sheet (left) is dated 9/53 and the colour two-pager (folding from top) was current at the time of the 1954 Motor Show.

Green-tinted monochrome artwork characterises these 9/54 and 6/55 printings of a catalogue for the 'facelifted' 1954–56 Series II Minor – this time including the Traveller. The twice-folded single sheet gives an 11 x 8½ inch landscape format.

Full-colour artwork features in this late Series II catalogue (date 9/55), which establishes a new format for Minor catalogues: a single 22 x 25 inch sheet with two horizontal folds and one vertical fold, reducing to regular 11 x 8¹/2 inch size.

The fully opened out three-strip spread of the Series II catalogue dated 9/55 shows its charming, well-detailed artwork.

Typical of parsimonious Nuffield/BMC, the Series II artwork was retouched so that it could be re-used (with a new cover image) for the 1956–57 offerings for the Minor 1000 – in English and foreign-language versions. Differences for the Minor 1000 catalogue include the addition of glovebox lids, a different steering wheel, chrome instead of painted rear lamp plinths, and the deletion of the armrests on the rear door of the four-door saloon.

Chapter Six

The
Morris Major

The Major's launch catalogue played on the Minor's reputation, and used stereotypical Australian beach scenes. But the Holden kicked sand in BMC's face.

WHICH CAR SET the British motor industry in Australia on the road to ruin? There's a strong case for arguing that it's the Morris Major, kissing Australian cousin of the Minor.

You're excused if you haven't heard of this antipodean curiosity, which probably rates as one of BMC's more obscure vehicles, but it's basically a modified Wolseley 1500 – in other words a Morris Minor in a party frock.

From Minor to Major

The Major was the product of one of the most convoluted development programmes in BMC's history. The design can be traced back to the original 1951 mock-ups for a restyled Minor described in Chapter Four. As discussed, these ultimately evolved into a proposal by long-time Austin styling chief Dick Burzi for a rebodied Minor, to be built on a modified Minor floorpan and to be powered by a 1200cc version of the BMC B-series engine.

By this stage, however, around the end of 1955, circumstances had changed. The car would offer little over the revised 948cc Minor, and would risk having a relatively short life before being displaced by a new Issigonis design of some description. It was therefore decided to move the 'New Minor' upmarket, with luxury trim and a larger, 1500cc engine, and sell it as the Wolseley 1500 and the Riley One-point-Five. The original Morris variant, however, was put into production in Australia, and launched in March 1958 as the Morris Major.

The Major Mk I – and its Austin sister

Externally identical to the Wolseley

and now a lusty big brother for the famous **MINOR**

THE SPECTACULAR NEW MORRIS Major

The Austin Lancer Mk I
used a slightly
modified version of the
Wolseley 1500 grille,
and recalled that of the
A35. The 'lightning
flash' front chrome
strip echoed that of
the Austin A55 Mk I.
(Don Salter)

How it all started: the
'Minor 1200' (that's
what the badges say)
photographed in two-
door form in 1957.
(BMIHT/Rover)

Mock-up for a 'New
Minor' two-door
estate, photographed
in 1956. (BMIHT/Rover)

A four-door estate was also tried, and this mock-up features a different treatment on each side. The conventional sixth light on the opposite side to the camera seems a better solution than the more radical suggestion in full view. (BMIHT/Rover)

1500, apart from a simplified grille and a revised lamp configuration, the Major – billed as 'the friendly family car' – was also mechanically the same, and differed only in having a more spartan interior. There was also an Austin version, the Lancer, with a vertical Austin grille replacing the upright Wolseley item and with the Morris's central instrument panel relocated in front of the driver.

Burzi's team developed a two-door variant, and they also mocked up various estates, but neither of these potential additions to the range saw production. Nor were the Major and Lancer introduced in Britain, as BMC's PR men suggested would happen. It does seem, however, that a 'Morris 1200' version of the Major came very close to being launched on the British market.

The Mk II Major and Lancer

In July 1959 the two cars were substantially revised. The wheelbase was extended by 6 inches and the rear remodelled to take American-style fins and a larger squared-off boot; overall length was up 9 inches. Frontal styling was also made more angular and on the Lancer was revised to make the Austin look not unlike the Farina A55 Mk II. The story goes that there was never going to be a Mk II Lancer, but that pressure from Austin dealers forced one to be cobbled together at the last moment.

In addition to the restyling, dampers (still lever-arm) were uprated, wider wheels fitted, and the body beefed up with extra box sections; the interior was also restyled and the cars given a front bench seat, with the handbrake on the right. The 50bhp 1489cc B-series engine remained as before, but the rear axle ratio was lowered, to give a little extra acceleration.

Stillborn developments

Had the stylists and – presumably – the product-planners not reined themselves in, the revamping of the Major and Lancer wouldn't have stopped there. Not only was a more outlandish frontal treatment proposed, but in addition a four-door estate was put together, as a fully operational prototype. The idea of a compact four-door estate was clearly

What had those BMC stylists been snacking on? This outlandish proposal dates from 1957 and at least has the virtue of balancing out the elongated rear of the Mk II cars. The grille has undertones of Studebakers of the period. (BMIHT/Rover)

Surely a sensible idea? This estate version of the Major Mk II would have stood a good chance of pulling in decent sales in Australia. But it never reached production. (BMIHT/Rover)

an attractive one in Australia, as French manufacturer Simca also came up with an Aronde with this style of body, specifically for Australia. Unlike the Morris, however, the Simca offering entered production.

The Major Elite

In early 1961, de luxe versions of the Lancer and Major were announced. These had more chrome, revised two-tone paint schemes, and improved equipment levels. The final development of the Major (but not of the Lancer – that was deleted) came in April 1962, when it received a Zenith-carb 58bhp 1622cc engine and telescopic rear dampers, as well as a restyled grille and interior. Known as the Major

Elite, it lasted until spring 1964, when it was replaced by the Australian-built Morris 1100.

Behind the wheel of a Series II

Once you've got over the bizarre pastiche-American styling, inside and out, and have settled into the upright bench seat and started up, you're on familiar ground – a Wolseley 1500 owner would soon feel at home.

Still, the interior is a bit of a culture shock, with its pressed-metal dashboard housing rather cheap-and-nasty round dials and stylised square plastic knobs, and the slim BMC steering column sheathed in a very transatlantic-looking shroud. As for the furnishings, there's rubber matting on the floor, while seats and door trims are in some of the toughest and most utilitarian vinyl you're likely to encounter on a car of this era.

Under way, there's that characteristic B-series engine tone, solid and sturdy, and the gearchange is pure rear-wheel-drive BMC – slightly loose but reason-ably precise, with no synchro on bottom and that on second fading fast. The 1500's hydraulic clutch is also familiar; satisfactorily weighted, it engages far more smoothly than the short-travel and often juddery rod-actu-ated clutch of the Minor. As for the brakes, they are to big-drum Wolseley specification, and are smooth, progressive, and effective.

Not surprisingly, considering its power-to-weight ratio, the 19cwt Major is distinctly leisurely in picking up speed. In fact it feels less sprightly than a 1098cc Minor. Once wound up, though, it will settle at a relaxed 60mph with rather less commotion than its younger sister, and with somewhat more in reserve – maximum speed is around 80mph. Where the Major really scores is in its low-down torque – it pulls like a tractor, and can go down almost to walking pace in third gear.

These characteristics – leisurely acceleration but impressive low-end torque and relaxed cruising – are exactly those that made Australia's Holden, with its unstressed small 'six', so very successful.

Bizarre, really: the front and rear ends of the restyled Major Mk II fail to marry with the curved centre section. (Paul Debois/Classic and Sports Car)

Despite skinny cross-plies and a leaf-sprung rear axle, the Major feels safe and reassuring, although it corners with more roll than a Minor. Thanks to the excellent Morris rack-and-pinion steering it also makes up in responsiveness what it lacks in ultimate adhesion.

Although the ride is still fairly firm, it feels more absorbent than on the Minor, and the uprated damping is certainly more effective. The chassis in fact really gives the impression of having been sorted to suit Australian roads, and thanks to the extra rigidity conferred by those supplementary box sections it feels impressively solid and all-of-a-piece on bad surfaces. Again this sturdy and unbreakable feel makes one think of the unsubtle but tough Holden.

In isolation, then, the Major feels about right for the market at which it was aimed. This point deserves emphasis, because the Major was pretty much a flop for BMC and — as already men-

Ersatz American styling of the rear recalls what Austin did with the Austin A55 Mk I, and Standard with the Vanguard Phase III – all rather sad, in retrospect. (Paul Debois/Classic and Sports Car)

The Series II Major/Lancer dashboard was bare and somewhat Ford-like.

tioned — can have laid at its door much of the blame for the ultimate demise of BMC/BL in Australia. How come?

Holden sets the pace

At the formation of BMC, Austin and Nuffield cars dominated the Australian market. Between them they held a 30.4 per cent share in 1951, as Empire loyalty, a scarcity of American dollars, and the policy of Imperial Preference kept out the previously popular American cars.

But the market was a rapidly expanding one, and one not likely to be bound by Empire ties if more suitable vehicles from elsewhere came along — especially if those vehicles were to be of an all-Australian make.

A mystery Australian Minor

The decision to make a special Australian small Morris with B-series power seems not to have been a last-minute one: Morris board meeting minutes from January 1956 talk of a '1200cc Morris Minor with cam steering', describing this model as an 'Australian version to suit the Australian market'. However, whether these initial thoughts were for a modified standard Minor or for a version of the Burzi 'New Minor', deprived of its steering rack, is not clear. And why go to the bother of dispensing with the excellent Minor rack-and-pinion steering?

As much as anything, this was because, as elsewhere in the world, British vehicles, frantically exported under government pressure, soon proved themselves less than ideally suited to 'colonial' conditions. Weakly suspended Austins and Standards, further hobbled by unsatisfactory after-sales support, were a poor foundation for future expansion. Nor were matters going to change with the arrival of local assembly, despite BMC's substantial investment in new plant for its Australian operations.

And so, as the General Motors Holden established itself, buyers began to turn away from BMC. Holden's market share rose from 23 per cent in 1951 to 41.7 per cent in 1957, while BMC's share fell to 17.5 per cent.

Quite simply, the Holden was the sort of car Australians wanted. Once initial problems, such as a lack of body rigidity, had been tackled, it rapidly became an Australian institution. With no real competition, it became entrenched in the market, as high volume kept prices down and made it difficult for any would-be challenger to become established.

What price a 'British Holden'?

BMC sat back and let this happen. Yet as early as 1950 Lord Nuffield, always keenly interested in the Australian market, had recognised the threat posed by the Holden. On his orders a Holden was shipped back to Cowley. Charles Griffin, later to become Chief Engineer at Cowley, and thus the man responsible for the Major's engineering, recalls Nuffield — whom he remembers as 'a very wise old bird' — telling him 'that's the sort of car we should be making'.

This was not an unfamiliar tune: in 1947 Lord Nuffield had cabled Cowley from Australia to state the urgent need for a six-cylinder vehicle to compete with those offered by other manufacturers. In 1948, too, consideration was given to a 'Coupé Express' 15cwt pick-up based on the Morris Six — a 'ute' of this sort being just the thing the Australians loved.

The snag was that to produce a Holden rival would demand a substantial investment — not least in a new engine, as Nuffield's only small 'six' was the complex and unreliable overhead-cam unit found in the Morris Six and the Wolseley 6/80. To produce a car specifically for the then small Australian market simple didn't look viable — and doubtless also evoked memories of the catastrophic 'Empire Oxford' of the late 1920s. So Lord Nuffield's suggestion was taken no further.

In retrospect this appears a crucial mistake, as the investment would almost certainly have paid off in the longer term. In any case, what price a widened Morris Six with a simplified pushrod variant of its 2.2-litre ohc power unit? Such a car would even have looked a bit like the original 'Humpy Holden' . . .

Still, even as late as 1957 BMC retained sufficient strength in Australia for it to be able to mount a challenge to Holden – although as in Britain the situation was complicated by the combine having two major marques with their own dealerships and their own customer loyalties. There was also the obstacle of the great variety of models offered, dissipating effort and investment. One of Holden's great strengths was its one-model policy, emulating Volkswagen, which was BMC's other main rival in Australia.

BMC plans its counter-attack

By autumn 1957, when the Wolseley 1500 entered production at BMC's Sydney plant, it was clear that the firm was at last to confront the problem. The factory had been newly expanded, and equipped with the latest machinery, and had the capacity to produce 50,000 cars per annum, rising to 100,000. This was when the total Australian market was around 155,000, so when BMC began talking of an all-new '100 per cent Australian' car, it was immediately presumed that it had a pretty exciting product up its sleeve. Expectations were further boosted when Leonard Lord announced his intention to take 30 per cent of the Australian market.

From expectation to disbelief

Thus began one of the longest-running farces in the history of the Australian motor industry, as feverish speculation began in the Australian press as to the nature of the new car. One London-based correspondent even reported that it was likely to be a stretched version of the Austin Metropolitan!

The May 1958 launch of the original Major and Lancer did nothing to lessen speculation: hadn't BMC said that the new car, when it came, would be totally different from existing models? The Major/Lancer, praised for its engine, criticised for its chassis behaviour, was clearly just as much of a stop-gap as the Morris Marshall, a Morris-badged Austin A95 that BMC had launched the year before.

A mystery car with 'hydraulic suspension' (presumably Issigonis's XC9001, which eventually evolved into the Austin 1800) was reported at MIRA. Was this the new Australian car? Or

Two brochure images show how the frontal treatment of the Major changed from the Mk I to the Mk II: a different grille, different light nacelles, revised bumpers, and a flatter bonnet without a mascot characterise the be-finned Mk II.

The Lancer Mk II has a
front seemingly
cobbled up from
whatever was left in
the Austin parts-bin.

was it the Farina-styled prototype (in fact the Austin A99) caught by a 'scoop' photographer? Or would the car be a 1½-litre derivative of the exciting new Austin A40? Even *The Autocar* got in on the act, talking of the Australian car possibly being fitted with Flexitor rubber suspension as used on the recently launched Austin Gipsy.

All this fun and games came to a rather pathetic end with the introduction of the Series II Major and Lancer. Was this all BMC's ballyhoo amounted to – a titivated Wolseley 1500? With Ford and Chrysler both planning big investments in Australia, and VW mopping up the small-car market, surely BMC couldn't be serious?

When it had recovered from its disappointment, the Australian press was in fact quite nice about the Series II. *Modern Motor*, for example, judged it 'the most improved car of the year'.

The problem, though, was that the public didn't much like the thing: in 1960 BMC sold only 11,045 Majors and Lancers, while Volkswagen sold almost 18,000 Beetles and GM-H knocked out 107,690 Holdens.

The Major wasn't a bad car, especially in its final Elite form ('hard to beat – both as value for money and as a car that gets you places quickly and is a pleasure to drive', wrote *Modern Motor*). Despite its impressive performance, it simply wasn't a Holden rival, though, and for the price of a Major you could buy a two-year-old Holden off any secondhand car lot in the country.

Nor was it a serious competitor to the VW, as had been intended, since it was both more expensive and less sophisticated. This at least might have changed had Charles Griffin had his way. The independent rear end designed by Jack Daniels for use in the Minor was offered by Griffin to the Australians for possible use on the Major. But presented with the choice of either this set-up, with its semi-trailing arms and transverse laminated torsion bar, or the existing leaf-sprung live axle, the Australian management chose the cheaper live axle.

As the Sydney plant had been equipped by 1958 with all the new tooling necessary to build a fully indigenous design, the Major (96 per cent Australian content by the time of the Elite) constituted a disturbing miscalculation. 'The Major was ill-conceived and badly contrived,' admits Charles Griffin. 'We couldn't succeed [in Australia] making the cars we were making.'

Too little, too late

After this fiasco, it was expected that BMC would reappraise its policies, and finally launch what was really needed – a genuine competitor for the Holden. This eventually happened in May 1962, by which time industry-watchers were in despair, as Ford's Australian-built Falcon was by then well-established and Chrysler's Valiant had just been introduced, while all BMC was offering was the Austin A60 – a local 1622cc development of the be-finned A55 – and a basically identical Morris Oxford.

BMC's answer to the Holden was called the Austin Freeway or, in luxury trim, the Wolseley 24/80. It was

A surviving Major Elite displays its new horizontal-slat grille. From the side the extended tail and bluff front look pretty risible. (Author)

essentially an A60 powered by a 2.4-litre six-cylinder variant of the 'B' series engine. Despite favourable reviews and competitive pricing, the two models, replacing the A60/Oxford, were another failure for the company.

It was a sad case of 'too little, too late', a situation that can be directly attributed to the decision to produce the Major. If the Freeway had gone into production in 1958/59 instead of the Major, at a time when BMC was still reasonably strong in Australia, and

before it had to contend with the aggressively marketed Falcon and Valiant, by 1962 it could have evolved into a genuinely effective rival to the Holden, Ford and Chrysler — perhaps even with a V8 derivative, as planned at one stage. As it was, the Freeway of 1962 looked dated and frumpy and, in Charles Griffin's opinion, 'there was no way it could be successful'.

But by this time both the Freeway and the Major were very much yesterday's cars. Spurred on by its phenomenal success with the Mini, BMC-Australia saw its future as being in compact front-wheel-drive cars. Accordingly it gave up the attempt to compete with Holden, abandoning a scheme for a modified V8-powered Freeway and shelving a later project for an all-new V8 car.

By 1974 BL was dead in Australia. The success of the fwd cars had proved ephemeral, with well-conceived attempts to update them being too late to salvage their position in the market. The P76 of 1973 arrived too late, after a seven-year gestation period, to redress the situation for a demoralised concern riven with industrial strife — and that was without considering the unlovely big saloon's clumsy styling and lousy quality. Is it fanciful to trace this ultimate débâcle back to the decision to produce the Morris Major?

Chapter Seven

The Alta conversion

IF YOU WANTED more 'go' from your side-valve Minor back in the 1950s, there was one solution that stood apart: the Alta overhead-valve conversion, latterly retailed by tuning king Vic Derrington.

Bathing in the reflected competitions glory of Geoffrey Taylor's Alta concern, this was no crude and half-baked ohv add-on. Given Taylor's expertise with twin-cam racing engines, it's no surprise that the conversion was notably well-conceived, and that it featured an alloy cylinder head; perhaps slightly eyebrow-raising, however, was that with twin carbs and a racing exhaust manifold, a race-tuned and fully balanced Alta-powered Minor could clock 0–50mph in 9 seconds, and was supposedly good for over 90mph. For £45, plus a modest £4 for fitting, you could start the transformation of your matronly Moggy into something altogether more tigerish . . .

Geoffrey Taylor and Alta

The Alta story goes back to 1927, when a young engineer in Kingston-upon-Thames, Surrey, decided to build his own sports car – from scratch. The man was Geoffrey Taylor, then working as a sub-contract machinist for the nearby ABC car company. By November 1928 the car was complete, down to a Taylor-designed-and-built all-aluminium twin-cam 1074cc engine – quite an achievement given that the

work was all carried out in the stable block of the family home. The car was named Alta, after a town in Alberta, Canada, which Taylor had come across in a novel he had been reading.

After various competition successes, Taylor set up the Alta Car & Engineering Company Ltd in January 1931, and between then and 1935 he built 12 Alta '1100' sports cars. He also devised his own Roots-type superchargers and developed an improved 1500cc version of his engine; from these activities sprang a run of six 1500cc racers, and seven road-going sports cars – some supercharged and some with a 2-litre engine. The ultimate pre-war Altas followed: three supercharged racers with all-independent sliding-pillar suspension. The best of these was capable of giving the works 2-litre ERA a run for its money.

Developing the Ford V8 for marine use helped keep the Tolworth works busy, as did government contract work, while a further earner was the manufacture of aluminium cylinder heads for cars such as the Austin Seven, the original 1920s/'30s side-valve Morris Minor, and the Triumph Seven. Much in demand, the Alta head for the Austin was revived after the war, and clearly showed the potential for bolt-on tuning gear for popular cars.

Post-war, Taylor built a small series of supercharged $1^1/_2$-litre Grand Prix cars, and from these he developed in 1952/53 a 2-litre unsupercharged car

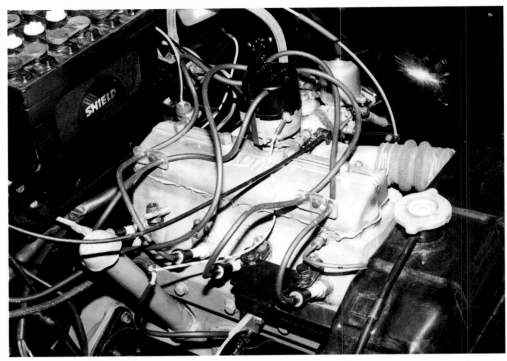

for Formula 2; the unblown 2-litre also powered the successful HWM racers. It was not the Alta F2s, however, that thrust the Tolworth firm to prominence; rather it was the use of Alta engines not only by HWM but also by local firm Connaught. In 2½-litre form the Alta engine, which traced its design back to the original unit of 1927/28, powered the B-series Grand Prix Connaught, and it was this car, driven by Tony Brooks, that achieved the historic victory at the Syracuse GP in 1955 which marked the beginning of Britain's re-establishment at the forefront of F1 racing.

Connaught was never going to be a long-term player, though, and in 1956, after completing a last batch of 2½-litre engines, Geoffrey Taylor, by now dogged by ill-health, closed down the Alta works. By this time, however, Alta had diversified into the Morris ohv head, which had been launched in 1954. Surprisingly, few writers bother to mention this in their reviews of Alta history, despite an estimated production of around 2,000 heads.

Alta by Derrington

With the closure of Alta, rights to the Austin Seven head and the Morris ohv conversion passed to V. W. Derrington, down the road in Kingston. Famed from Brooklands days as a purveyor of go-faster bits, Derrington marketed the Morris conversion until the mid-1960s, although inevitably with fewer and fewer buyers as time went on. It seems that at some stage former sports car manufacturer HRG took over manufacture on behalf of Derrington. Apparently it made only a few batches, alongside its own HRG crossflow head for the B-series BMC engine.

The Alta head for the Minor

The 1954 introduction of the Morris conversion might seem as if Alta had missed the boat; after all, the pushrod A-series Austin engine had been a standard fit in the Minor since the beginning of the previous year. It wasn't quite that simple, though. With most Minors exported in the car's early years, it was only as the '50s progressed that enthusiasts started to have access in any numbers to affordable secondhand Minors – and that meant sidevalve MMs.

Additionally, as John Bolster of *Autosport* highlighted in his December '54 review of the Alta head, the 803cc SII was hardly a solution to the Minor's power deficit. 'Since [the MM's introduction] the makers have come across with an ohv unit, but as this is appre-

This Alta head has a period twin-SU conversion with a 'bunch of bananas' tubular exhaust manifold and a substantial steel air-cleaner assembly. (Graham Holt)

ciably smaller than the old one, it is not very much faster. Furthermore, the gearbox that goes with the new motor is not as pleasant as the original,' he wrote. Hence the appeal of the Alta head. 'At once one has the bigger engine, the better gearbox, and an efficient head that will really extract some power from it. Bench tests have proved that the output of the unit is, in fact, almost doubled.'

The same arguments still applied after the 1956 introduction of the Minor 1000. If you couldn't reach to one of these, there was no point even contemplating the work involved in fitting one of the new 948cc engines to your old MM, said Derrington. The Alta head was 'a far better proposition' and, he claimed, 'develops slightly more power than a standard 1000 engine'; backing this up, he quoted an output of 38bhp for an Alta-Minor with standard carburetter and standard exhaust. This was good enough, he said, to raise maximum speed from 62mph to 75mph, and reduce 30–50mph acceleration in top gear from 31.6 to 17.2 seconds.

That was only the start. Add a twin-SU conversion and Derrington's 'Deep Note Exhaust System' (this last boosting power by a claimed 15–20 per cent) and power rose to 44bhp — for an extra outlay of £31 5s 0d. Substitute an extractor-type racing exhaust manifold, and you could dispose of 49bhp and an 89mph claimed maximum speed. The ultimate race-tuned engine, with 9.5 to 1 compression ratio, extractor-type exhaust manifold, larger inlet valves and bigger SUs, was good for 'over 52bhp' and a 94mph top speed 'under favourable circumstances'. Total cost of this kit was £93 15s 0d — excluding the full balancing of the bottom end, which was highly desirable if the power unit was not to fly apart under its newly doubled output. Also suggested was moving to a higher back axle ratio of 4.22 to 1, a suitable differential being available through Derrington's.

The Alta engine in use

Was the conversion reliable? No reputation for unreliability has filtered down through the years, and in its day it was well regarded by the Derrington mechanics who installed many of the cylinder heads.

Inevitably age and a failure to use corrosion inhibitors has resulted in many heads suffering serious corrosion. A failure to observe regular oil changes can also lead to problems, by causing clogging of the restrictor pin on the oil-delivery pipe feeding oil to the rockers; conversely, over-lubrication results if the pin is omitted.

But in essence the design is sound, with possibly the only area of weakness being the lightweight pushrods: it's not unknown for these to bend.

Derrington took pains, in fact, to reassure customers about the sturdiness of the conversion. 'The Alta conversion has proved to be exceptionally efficient and reliable, and lengthy use has in no way reduced the reliability of the engine or resulted in excessive wear,' he stated in his publicity. 'Periods of up to 30,000 miles have been covered without the necessity of a rebore or reground crankshaft, whilst the many successes in racing testify to the soundness of the design,' he continued — casting on the way an interesting perspective on '50s expectations of engine durability. These days, thanks to modern oils, and with the fitment of an auxiliary oil filter, an engine life of more than 30,000 miles should be more than feasible . . .

How it goes

Contemporary reports confirm the effectiveness of the Alta conversion. Particularly enthusiastic was John Bolster's 1954 *Autosport* test of racing driver Alan Foster's Alta-Minor, an experience dubbed as 'exhilarating'. Interestingly, this was with a single-carb installation, Bolster writing that no advantage was to be gained by fitting a twin-SU conversion – a Taylor-era opinion at odds with that of Vic Derrington, who felt twin carbs gave an additional 4–6bhp.

'I found that, providing the revs were kept up, the little vehicle was very lively in traffic, and as soon as I reached the open road I settled down to a cruising speed well above the original maximum. The engine is no noisier than standard, though the exhaust has a rather more powerful note during hard acceleration,' reported Bolster.

'The performance is improved out of all recognition, and I was at last able to make full use of that outstanding road-holding. Travelling three-up, I was able to *average* close on 60mph for quite a long cross-country journey. The incredulity on the faces of some of the people I passed had to be seen to be believed.'

Bolster recorded an averaged-out maximum of 76.5mph – 'a colossal speed for a one-litre four-seater saloon'

– and clocked 0–50mph in 13.4 seconds, with 60mph coming up in 20.4 seconds. These figures were with a corrected speedo: at a genuine flat-out 78mph the Minor's optimistic instrument read an impress-your-neighbours 86mph.

Fuel consumption with a rich needle fitted hit a low of 24mpg with sustained high-speed cruising, but fell to around 30mpg at a 65mph cruise. On a weaker needle, said Bolster, up to 45mpg was claimed by Alta. Meanwhile *The Motor*, softer-pedalling, found that at lower speeds the Alta-Minor was actually more economical than the side-valve, and that consumption only fell towards 30mpg in very fast driving.

Over in the States, *Sports Cars Illustrated* magazine had an MM converted. The result, it said, was that Nuffield's 'Delightful Dud' was transformed into 'a buzzing, MG-hunting tiger'. Admittedly the car ran twin SUs and a proprietary Huth exhaust manifold and big-bore exhaust, and also had the further tweaks of a 60-thou over-

Vic Derrington's Alta-head MM leads a Standard Ten and a Ford Anglia 100E in the March 1956 BARC Members' Meeting at Goodwood. (Charles Dunn)

bore, lightweight pistons and rods, and some careful porting, but this was hardly ultra-radical. The figures spoke for themselves: 0–50mph acceleration dropped from 21.7 to 10.4 seconds, with a 0–60mph time of 14.7 seconds against a standard-spec time of 38.6. Maximum speed was up from 62.7mph to 84.3mph. Were the boys on the team impressed? You bet.

'. . . the whole character of the automobile has changed,' the magazine reported. 'Cornering is now even better than before, thanks to the new horsepower . . . Gear shifting has been cut in half in city and normal country driving, and hill climbing has become a pleasure instead of a terror. The engine will rev to 6000rpm and can pull better than 5500rpm in high. Performance is so much improved that it is almost unbelievable, especially since the whole car is also smoother than ever before . . . We have even found that in average driving the gas mileage has gone up, not down, by two or three miles per gallon.'

Standard MM v Alta-Minor

Everything you might have read is true: the Alta conversion really does transform the Minor. Thanks to owners Sandy and Rosie Hamilton, the author convincingly established this when he carried out a back-to-back trial of their standard and Alta-headed Minors.

The standard MM never ceases to surprise with the performance it can muster. Despite being no lighter than the Morris Eight Series E, it seems to manage rather better on the same modest side-valve engine. Perhaps superior aerodynamics has something to do with it.

All the same, the MM is always on the margins. While it will bowl along on a level road at a contented and refined 50mph, even with foot flat to the floor you're working the car to exceed that speed. Hit a slope that's against you, and speed will fall right away, although the low-down torque means that the car will lug slowly up.

The Alta-Minor is a different beast entirely – and this is with a standard single SU and a standard manifold. In the same way as the Wolseley Eight ohv engine, it's instantly responsive, revving crisply and delivering its power with no hint of sluggishness. With an alloy head and two-piece pushrods, there's a metallic quality to the soundtrack lacking in the more plodding all-iron side-valve engine, but it's never displeasing.

You're soon cruising at 45–50mph, on a much smaller throttle opening than the standard car, and at 55mph you're still accelerating. At that speed in a normal MM you'd as likely as not be on full throttle and timing your acceleration by the calendar.

Take to more hilly terrain and the Alta-powered Minor will climb comfortably, perhaps still putting on speed, when the side-valve car is running out of puff and demanding a downchange. If speed has been shaved off, though, it's quickly put back on again once you're on the level.

On give-and-take roads the Alta-Minor allows you to go as fast as you'd safely go in any later A-series Minor, whereas the MM is all too prone to holding up following traffic. Were the Alta car even mildly tuned, the results would be even more impressive. As it is, you can see why the conversion was so popular.

The Alta kit

So what did you get for your money – £43 10s in 1954, rising to £52 10s in 1961 – when you bought an Alta head for your Minor? Quite a bit, if you break it all down.

The key component is of course the head, which is cast in 'Birmidal' aluminium alloy with 'Brico' hardened valve seats, and which is blessed with an 8.7 to 1 compression ratio – or 9.5 to 1 (with stronger valve springs) when to 'racing' specification. Originally sold ready-assembled, the head uses double valve springs, has inlet valves a little larger than standard MM-size, and features a set of cast-iron rockers on a shaft lubricated by a special external oil line. The head is topped by a smart cast-alloy rocker cover, secured by four large brass socket-bolts.

Linking the side-valve camshaft to the new inclined overhead valves are two-part pushrods comprising short lower 'inter-tappets' and equally short upper pushrods. The 'inter-tappet' takes the place of the original valve, and rests on top of the tappet; its top features a socket in which the ball-end of the new Alta pushrod engages. With the old inlet and exhaust ports now redundant, these are covered by a large steel side-plate that replaces the normal pressed-steel cover used to gain access to the tappets.

Other conversion parts include a cast-iron adaptor to allow the exhaust to mate with the exhaust manifold, which post-conversion sits an inch or two higher. Similarly, the distributor is now higher-mounted, so a lengthened shaft is provided. A special water outlet housing, with or without thermostat provision, is also included, and finally there is an alloy plate that fits between the carburetter and the

The Alta head was cast in 'Birmidal' aluminium alloy, with suitably hardened valve seats. The inlet valves are a little larger than on a regular MM side-valve. (Author's collection)

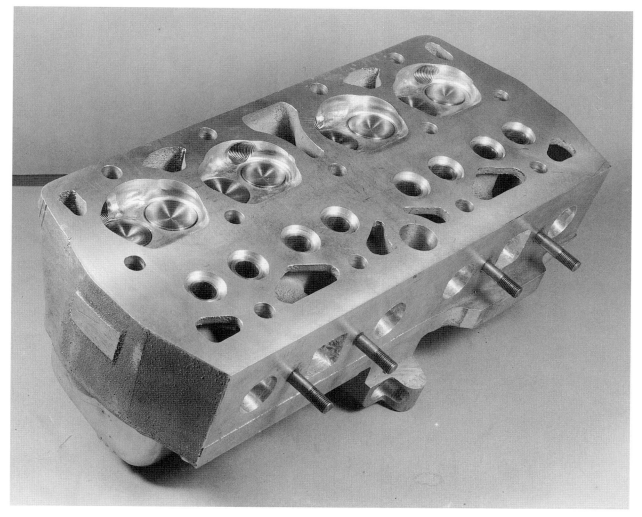

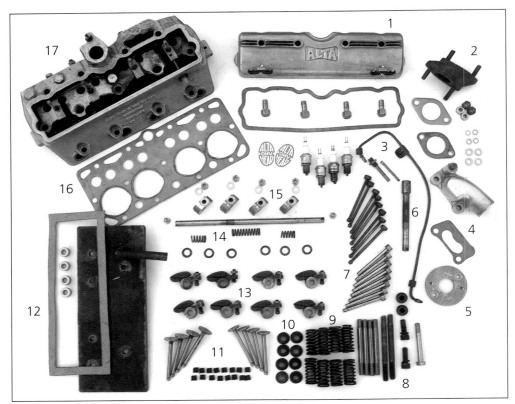

1　Rocker Cover
2　Exhaust adapter
　　and gaskets
3　Oil feed pipe for
　　rockers
4　Water outlet and
　　gasket
5　Carb/air cleaner
　　adapter
6　Distributor shaft
7　Split pushrods
8　Replacement
　　cylinder head studs
9　Valve springs
10　Valve spring clips
11　Valves and cotters
12　Blanking plate for
　　old tappet chest
13　Rockers
14　Rocker shaft and
　　springs
15　Rocker shaft
　　clamps
16　Head gasket
17　Cylinder head

The Alta conversion,
fully dismantled. The
key identifies the
principal components.
(Tony Baker)

The fully-assembled
head, showing the
generous depth of the
alloy casting and the
sturdy rocker
mechanism. (Tony
Baker)

air cleaner (presuming the standard carb is retained) and which rotates the air cleaner downwards in order that it does not foul the bonnet. If the MM is a car without a water pump, and thus with the dynamo bracket integral with the side-valve head, also needed will be a special dynamo bracket; this bolts to the two front cylinder-head studs.

There is no cause to change the distributor if the car has a Lucas DKYH4A/40251 unit; however, if it has a 176A/10333A distributor this will need to be replaced by a DKYH4A/40251.

Fitting the Alta conversion

Most customers chose to have Derrington's fit their heads, recalls long-time employee Ted Napper. 'The heads came to us all ready to fit, and neatly boxed-up. But quite a few went for polishing and modifying. In particular I remember we used to reshape the combustion chambers to give more squish.'

Fitting the head, says Napper, was a bit of a job. 'There was a lot of work involved. But once you'd got it right, it really was quite an improvement, especially with the twin SUs we put on most of the engines we converted.'

The first stage in installation is to clean thoroughly the exterior of the engine. This done, the cylinder head is removed; then all but the four short offside studs are extracted. Following this, the manifold with its carburetter is removed, and the valves and springs.

The pistons are then decarbonised, keeping a ring of carbon at the outer circumference as is normal decoke practice, and the top face of the block fully cleaned.

The Alta studs can now be screwed in, and the replacement distributor shaft inserted.

All carbon must now be scrupulously removed from the side-valve valve ports, after which the 'inter-tappets', duly oiled, can be inserted through the valve-guide holes. The existing tappet screws are screwed two turns inwards, but not locked, then the gasket and the

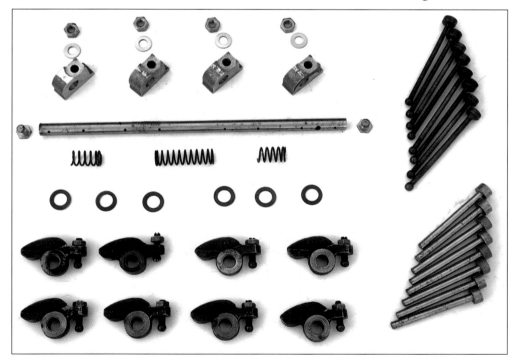

The valve actuation gear. From top to bottom are: rocker-shaft mounting brackets; rocker-shaft, rocker-shaft springs with washers, and rocker-shaft closing bolts; rockers. To the right are the two-piece pushrods: the lower bundle comprises eight 'inter-tappets' with cupped tops and the upper bundle comprises eight short pushrods with ball ends to engage in the 'inter-tappet' cups. (Tony Baker)

head itself can be fitted and torqued down; this process includes installing two Allen-head bolts that go through the inlet ports. First, though, before fitting the head the installer should clean the top face of the head again, and pour a little engine oil into each bore.

Australia's answer to the Alta

The Australians had their own ohv conversion for the MM – although they could obtain Alta heads if they wanted. The home-grown kit was offered by A. J. Mazengarb of St Mary's, New South Wales. Very different from the Alta conversion, it positioned the carburetters (assuming two SUs were used) on the offside, along with the exhaust manifolding and the water outlet; the dynamo also changed sides from the offside to the nearside. It is not known for how long this conversion was made, but advertisements can be found in 1954 Australian motoring magazines.

As in England, there were other tuning options available. Kleinig Products offered a 'Super High-Power Dome Cylinder Head', which appears to be similar to the alloy Derrington 'Silvertop' head sold in Britain, while Victoria-based Monaro Motors could provide twin-carb conversions and a lot more. In fact Monaro offered 'off the shelf' new MMs equipped with twin carbs, a tuned engine, and a special 'low pressure' silencer.

Next the pushrods are inserted and the rocker-shaft assembly fitted, following which the side-valve tappets are adjusted to .015–.020 inch and the tappet screws locked; the Alta sidecover can now be fitted, and the breather pipe connected to it.

At either end of the rocker-shaft are two set-bolts, and these must now be tightened, using one spanner against another. The Alta rockers can now be adjusted to their .015 inch clearance.

The manifold and carburetter are now bolted back and the fuel line reconnected. A bit of oil over the valve gear, then the rocker cover can be fitted, after which the distributor is replaced and longer leads fitted; timing remains unchanged, but should be checked. As for plugs, long-reach Champion N5 or their Lodge or KLG counterparts were recommended; today a suitable plug would be a Champion N9Y or equivalent.

The rocker oil-pipe can now be fitted: an oil union replaces the bolt on the front camshaft bearing, and the pipe is then connected to this and to the union on the front offside of the cylinder head. A small bolt and a chamfered plate clamps the pipe to the top of a lug on the front of the head.

By this stage, little remains to be done. The exhaust can now be reconnected to the manifold, using the adaptor piece, and the carburetter re-installed; this will need re-needling. All the same, the air cleaner needs to be fitted at this juncture, and a small hole has to be drilled through the flange on the lower part of the cleaner, so the throttle return spring can be anchored.

The engine is now ready for firing-up, adjustment of the carburetter, and a short run – after which the cylinder-head nuts, and those for the sidecover and exhaust flange, should be tightened once more, with the engine cold.

Correct lubrication of the rocker-shaft is vital, and can be confirmed by the sight of oil exuding from the side of the rockers. A restrictor pin stops over-oiling, but it must be kept clean: after the first 100 miles and then every 500 miles it is recommended that the pin be pulled out and cleaned.

A freshly installed head should of course be re-torqued after a short while – Derrington's suggested after the first 100–200 miles.

The Alta conversion today

In 1973 Derrington's – which closed in 1986 – still had one loyal customer buying parts for the Minor conversion, and that year the remaining spares were sold to this gentleman. They didn't amount to much: by the time another enthusiast bought them in 1979 they came to 18 sets of rockers, two sets of pushrods, around 40 valves, two sets of rocker pedestals, five rocker shafts, and

15 steel head gaskets, plus a few other bits and bobs. What happened to any surplus heads, or bigger items such as rocker covers, is not known, any more than the fate of the tooling.

Today it is thought that around a dozen Alta-head Minors are still in use, but surviving heads are more numerous. Morris Minor Owners' Club Alta specialist Graham Holt runs a register, and at the last count had a total of 33 heads on his lists. More — probably many more — exist, but all too often they are incomplete or badly corroded. Be suspicious, therefore, of heads offered at surprisingly low prices: a complete conversion in good order is unlikely to be cheap these days, and there is a ready market for the heads.

Parts? Graham Holt has samples of almost all parts required, and as a mechanical engineer he has the skills necessary to create the drawings necessary for re-manufacture of components. A gasket specialist holds patterns for the head gasket, so these can be made up, while another Alta owner has commissioned the manufacture of some composite gaskets. Valve springs can be a problem, as the double springs used are not the same as those available for the normal Minor side-valve engine. The word is, however, that Austin Maxi 1500 double springs may do the job. With interest in Alta heads constantly rising, since the early 1980s, things can only improve as more examples emerge.

Chapter Eight

The Minor in the US

L OOK AT THE Minor's patchy performance in the States, and there's only one conclusion to draw: Nuffield and BMC blew it. Beaten to the export-sales punch by Austin, knocked reeling by Volkswagen, and in the end, thanks to sluggish model development, unable to pull itself up off the mat, the little Morris never fulfilled its potential.

Yet the Minor always had an appreciative – if select – following in the US, buoyed by a good press, and there were phases in its life when sales were relatively respectable. Today, too, it has a lively and enthusiastic Stateside fol-

lowing, and one that goes back a good many years.

The Minor's belated arrival in the US

In the early post-war years, resurgent and prosperous America was car-starved, and for a brief period, fuelled by a desperate need for dollars, British manufacturers lobbed anything with four wheels at the US market. For a while the Americans lapped it up, even if the vehicles were as patently unsuited to US use as the demure and weakly suspended Austin A40 Devon. Almost 10,000 Devons were sold in the States

Cal-look Minor? This smart yellow saloon runs a five-speed Datsun transmission with hydraulic clutch, and has servoed front disc brakes. (Tony Burgess)

in 1948, but as new American designs came on stream it was obvious that such a boom couldn't last.

At a Nuffield board meeting in March 1949 there was anguished hand-wringing at the reported fact that since the end of the war Austin had exported 15,000 vehicles to the US while Nuffield had only managed 1,773 – and 1,610 of those were MGs. Yet before Nuffield could redress the balance, it was recorded that demand in the States for small imports was falling rapidly.

The bubble was indeed bursting when Nuffield began its first hesitant shipments of the Minor, during 1949. During that year only 442 Minors reached the States – chicken-feed, especially when you realise that nearly 3,000 Minors hit Canada in '49. It was only in 1950 that exports to the US took off, with 2,126 Minors arriving there. This was a promising progression, especially as in November 1949 a depressed Nuffield board had discussed quitting the US market.

But in 1951 the Korean War knocked the company off balance, and in the prevailing atmosphere of grave crisis and severe material shortages Minor exports to the US dipped to 738 units. The following year shipments returned to a healthier 2,126 cars. But by that stage, despite the arrival of the ohv Series II, the Minor was too old-hat, too highly priced, and too punily motorised to have much appeal to a horsepower-crazed America in love with chromium plate, bigger-is-better, and fetishistic rocket-ship imagery.

Tell that to the Germans? Well, in fact the Volkswagen wasn't pushing many buttons either, at that time: compare the 887 Beetles sold Stateside in '52 with the 2,126 Minors unloaded that year. Hampered by a limited distribution network and a residual anti-German hostility, as well as by the car's extreme quirkiness, only 2,000-odd Beetles had been sold in the US by the end of 1953 – against three times that

number of Minors. But after Volkswagen had built up its position in Europe it would only be a matter of time before the same disciplined approach would be applied to the US market.

And so it transpired. As the Minor faded, so the Beetle imposed itself, thanks to the setting up of an exemplary sales and service organisation, and

The Americans like duo-toning: you'd never get way with this red-and-white car in Britain. (Jon Merker)

This stepside pick-up evokes a classic American idiom. (Jon Merker)

thanks to the VW's gathering reputation for unbreakable reliability. With Nuffield/BMC's legendary and ultimately suicidal casualness when it came to after-sales service, it took only until 1954 for annual Beetle sales to reach six times those of the Minor; in 1956 BMC sold fewer than 500 Minors in the States, while VW, with Volkswagen of America having been up and running since April 1955, achieved Beetle sales of 55,000 units.

The late '50s revival

It would be natural to assume, therefore, that the Minor was dead in the water by this time, as far as US sales were concerned. Extraordinarily, though, the Minor came back from the dead, and enjoyed a mid-life boom in the period 1957–61. Led by the Beetle, America fell in love with small imported motor cars.

Burgeoning prosperity brought not only two-car but three-car families, with housewives and student children wanting cheap, small and ideally chic

The things you find at the Waterford Pumpkin Festival car show! This oval-circuit racer has a 1598cc engine, provenance unknown but probably Japanese. (Glen Donaldson)

runabouts; at the same time a better-educated and more independent-minded generation of newly prosperous young people were keen to make their own value statement by rejecting Ma and Pa's Buick-is-Best ethos. So along with the MGAs, Triumph TRs and 356 Porsches, Young America discovered Beetles, Renault Dauphines . . . and Morris Minors.

In 1957, helped by the arrival of the considerably improved Minor 1000, Morris sales jumped nearly tenfold. In 1958 they doubled, to 9,076 units, and in 1959 they peaked at 14,991 cars. These figures are for all Morris cars; however, no SII/SIII Oxford or Isis models were sold in the States, so to all intents and purposes US Morris sales can be taken as meaning Morris Minor sales – except in 1959, when a certain number of 'Farina' Series V Oxfords were imported.

Detroit fights back

Come 1960, and the party was over. Detroit wasn't going to let foreigners

make the running in its own backyard, and for that model year Ford fielded its Falcon, Chrysler its Valiant, and GM its VW-aping rear-engined Corvair. Under attack from these low-priced 'compacts', the imports wilted. Morris sales at first held up reasonably well, with 10,788 cars sold in 1960, but 1961 sales of only 5,898 units told its own story; worse, most of the cars were relics from 1960 and even 1959 shipments. It was all over.

Yet imports continued, to special order, even when 1962 Morris sales of 934 units dipped to a wretched 348 sales in 1963 and a 'why bother?' 108

cars in 1965. Astonishingly, another revival then took place – at least up to a point. Led by the Japanese, small imports were reimposing themselves in the US market in the late '60s. Encouraged by this, financially floundering BMC shipped out 1,050 Minors in 1967, half going to the West Coast.

But the Minor was no Beetle, and it was too archaic to be any sort of competitor for the increasingly popular Datsuns and Toyotas. Limp advertising didn't help, and it took until well into 1968 to shift the modest 1967 consignment of cars. With emissions and safety regulations to meet, it was obviously not viable to continue with a US-market Minor nobody wanted to buy, so BMC concentrated instead on Federalising the front-wheel-drive 1300 into the Austin America, a venture that was – perhaps predictably – hardly much more successful.

Nineteen years after its US introduction, the Minor had thus reached the end of its Stateside career; in that time 56,640 Morris cars had been sold in the States, most of them Minors. At least 50 per cent of the Minors were two-door saloons, and most of the balance

convertibles: the Traveller had some following, but the van and pick-up were virtually unsaleable and tended to end up as works hacks for dealers and distributors.

'Lowlight' becomes 'highlight'

Nuffield and BMC never made much effort to tailor the Minor for US conditions. Flashing indicators only replaced trafficators from around 1952, and it was only towards the end of exports to the States that BMC deigned to fit a key lock for the (left-hand-side) driver's door – until then the driver had to unlock the passenger's door and either slide across or else flick the catch then get out and walk round to the other side of the car.

One modification was, however, forced on the Minor by US legislation: the headlamp height of the original 'lowlight' Minor did not meet US legal requirements introduced on 1 January 1949. Accordingly the 'highlight' wing configuration was hastily devised before imports began; Issigonis, as is well known, hated this corruption of his smooth-lined styling, which lopped

A bonnetful of V8, and then some: radical Mog at a '92 Palo Alto meeting. (Tony Burgess)

$1^1/_2$ mph from the car's already low top speed.

The wing modification was in fact something of a farce, and undoubtedly goes a good way towards explaining the slow start-up of US sales of the Minor. To get the car established, the first demonstrators for the States had hand-built wings. These added substantially to the Minor's cost, to the point of wiping out any profit. It seems that only 50 cars had hand-fabricated wings, but it was not until spring 1949 that output of pressed wings commenced, and even then these were not fully tooled panels.

By the end of March only 196 Morris cars had been shipped to the States, out of a target for the whole year of 5,000 vehicles. It was a month later that the decision was finally taken to tool up fully for the more economical mass-manufacture of the 'highlight' wings. This was because it was discovered that some Canadian territories were challenging the legality of the 'lowlight' configuration. With UK regulations also looking hostile, it was accordingly decided that by 'approximately 1951' all Minors would have the 'US pattern' front wings.

Another legal requirement stipulated twin rear lamps, with the result that early US-market Minors had pedestal-mounted round tail lamps rather than the single 'frenched' unit and its matching round reflector found on the first UK cars.

Minors in the US today

Today the US and Canadian Minor enthusiast is served by a trans-national club, the Morris Minor Registry of North America. According to administrator Tony Burgess, membership is now around 750, which at an average of $2^1/_2$ cars per member equates to around 2,000 Minors. 'There are probably a lot more about, but we've not been made aware of them,' says Burgess.

For many years the Minor movement was centred on California, where the first club, the Woodacre Woodies, was founded in 1973. Initially restricted to Travellers and the odd van or pick-up, by 1974 the Woodacre Woodies had joined the newly formed Morris Owners' Association of California. Meanwhile in New York the Morris Minor Registry had been set up, and in

---

Catastrophe in Canada

The viability of Minor sales in Northern America was somewhat questionable – at least in pre-BMC times. In September 1949 the devaluation of the pound triggered boardroom talk of being forced to sell the car in the US at 'flat cost'. A month later, when it was decided instead to take a 5 per cent profit, it was recorded that up until then the Minor had in fact been selling at a loss in the States. The headlamp fiasco must surely have at least in part accounted for this sorry state of affairs, which almost prompted Nuffield to withdraw the Morris marque from the States.

Worse was to occur in Canada. Thanks to restrictive economic policies, the Canadian car market collapsed in 1951 – just when the Korean War was causing more than enough difficulties for Morris. Stocks of unsold Minors and Oxfords piled up, and in July it was decided to ship 500 cars back to Britain. Despite being 'shop-soiled' and left-hand drive, they would be sold at a £200 premium.

By August it was calculated that at the then rate of sales Morris had two years' worth of stocks sitting in Canada. It was therefore decided to ship back 2,000 cars in all, mainly Minors and Oxfords. By the end of 1951 2,025 vehicles had been shipped home, with 3,141 remaining unsold in Canada. More re-importation was planned, but by spring 1952 the Canadian market had revived, and further shipments were cancelled.

All of which explains why Anders Clausager of BMIHT recently had to field a query from a perplexed British MM owner whose car appeared to be a Canadian-market car supplied new in Britain . . .

---

the Los Angeles area of California yet another grouping, Morris Minors Ltd, was in operation. By 1977 all three groups had merged into the Registry, which today has 36 regional officers but maintains a strong Californian representation.

This is not surprising. Minors were very much sold off the back of MG and Austin-Healey sports cars, and benefited

from the strong West Coast dealer network run by British Motor Car Distributors Ltd of San Francisco. On the East Coast, distribution was looked after by New York's J. S. Inskip, and in between there was precious little. That explains why most Minors are to be found either in California or the East Coast states of New England. At one stage, indeed, a good half of known survivors were California-domiciled, but growing Minor interest in other states, plus people moving east, has tipped that figure rather closer to a fifth these days.

Most cars are 1957–60 models, with MMs and SIIs being pretty rare. Two-doors are in the majority, with convertibles and Travellers being about evenly split. Four-doors are unusual. If 1954 import statistics are representative, the figures say it all: that year 161 two-doors, 116 Travellers and 120 tourers were shipped, but only 14 four-doors. A further indication is that the 1960 US catalogue refers to the four-door but doesn't bother to illustrate it.

Running a Minor in the States need not be a struggle. Both New York and California have Minor specialists, and there are two more in Oregon. Additionally, parts commonality with the Sprite/Midget is a big help – you're far more likely in the US to find one of these in a junkyard than a Minor.

Modified US Minors

As a result of the ready availability of Spridget parts, most people regularly using their Minor have fitted a Spridget 1275cc engine and gearbox, perhaps at the same time installing Spridget front disc brakes. Although this braking modification is considered old-hat in England – the brakes are small and the three-point fixing less than ideal – it is more readily achievable in the States than the Marina disc conversion: the Marina was only briefly imported to the

US and is rarely found these days.

Along with the 1275cc transplant, a higher-ratio Spridget differential is another popular modification, for less fussy freeway cruising. But that's usually where it stops, says Tony Burgess: telescopic dampers are rarely fitted, and chassis tend to stay largely standard.

Twin-cam Fiat engines? Oh no. With precious few Fiat 131s ever imported, the donor cars just aren't there, unless you get the chance to dismember a Fiat spider cheaply. Instead, transplant-happy Americans go for Nissan engine swaps. This is more of a West Coast thing, according to Burgess, and this is borne out by California-based Registry colleague Jon Merker, who reckons that nearly half the cars he knows have 1171cc or 1428cc Nissan drivetrains. These tend to come from the 1977–81 Nissan Sunny 210-series, the last Sunny models with rear-wheel drive.

Merker himself runs a 1275 Minor – 'I wanted to be able to get on and off California freeways' – but he says that the Nissan conversion is a dream ticket for US Minorists. 'The engine is almost a mirror image of the British unit, and it usually comes with either a five-speed or an automatic box.'

One of the leading proponents of 'Nee-san' Minors is Tony Martinis. 'The five-main-bearing Nissan A-series engine is great – it's indestructible, it has a superb alloy head, and Weber carbs will bolt straight on. If you take care of it, it'll outlive you, and even in stock form it'll really make a Minor move.'

Martinis says that the transplant isn't difficult. Installation details vary depending on personal preference and on the engine used, but in general the bulkhead ideally needs to be cut slightly, to move the engine back, or at the very least the radiator will require modifying and mounting further forward. To avoid having to tilt the engine/gearbox excessively downwards, a notch will also need to be cut in the bellhousing to clear the rack. Cutting back and reinforcing the front cross-member is advisable, too, so as to allow extra clearance. To mount the engine, Triumph Spitfire/GT6 mounts are used at the front, and a special crossmember is fabricated to support the gearbox.

Sprite/Midget discs and a telescopic conversion look after the front, possibly with an anti-roll bar, and at the back Martinis favours a Nissan pick-up or 710 station-wagon rear axle, with Minor spring mounts welded on in the correct position. 'These axles are unbustable, the right width, and have bigger and better brakes and bearings. They have six-stud hubs, so you need

Another California car, this pick-up runs a Chevy V8, coil-and-wishbone front end, and a narrowed rear axle on some serious rubber. (Tony Burgess)

It's tight! The Nissan installation in this van uses an A-series engine with a three-speed auto. A Weber carb is fitted, with manifolding from an early Nissan 1200 from the days before emission regs complicated things. The servo is an American unit, assisting a Midget disc set-up. (Tony Martinis)

to make an adaptor if you want to use Minor wheels, but that's not the end of the world . . .'

Martinis has the whole Nissan-Minor thing pretty sewn up, in fact, and sings loudly the praises of the more robust Japanese mechanicals – whether the ball-bearing clutch release or the beefier hubs and brakes. Drop in a VW Transporter petrol tank, nearly doubling fuel capacity, and you have one hell of a neat machine, he says.

His current transport? A pick-up powered by the special considerably strengthened engine used in Nissan forklift trucks. This J-type Nissan engine, found in less detuned form in many Nissan pick-ups, is a three-main-bearing iron-head unit available in various capacities. An MGB cylinder head, believe it or not, will fit straight on, as will an HRG-Derrington crossflow head, if you're really ambitious, and with Nissan tuning gear you can have a

real screamer of an engine. Fiat twin-cams, who needs them?

Any review of the American scene would be incomplete without a mention of V8 Minors. Surprisingly, perhaps, they're not that common: most of the readily available units are far too big and heavy. But there are a few Chevy-powered Minors to be found, usually toting '283' or '327' small-block V8s of one sort or another.

In general, then, it's either 1275cc A-series or pushrod Nissan power that characterises the non-standard Stateside Minor – and there are probably far fewer modified/uprated cars than in Britain. There's no denying, though, that it's a thriving scene these days in the States, and any West Coast or East Coast British car meet of reasonable size will have its contingent of Minors. It might not be a Beetle-sized cult, but the Morris Minor sure has a transatlantic following.

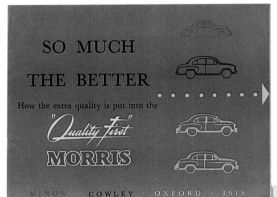

This 1956 Morris range catalogue for the 1957 model year (dated 12/56) showcases Cowley production processes, with banks of mono photos opposite artwork of the four models – Minor, Cowley 1500, Oxford Series III, Isis Series II. The cover line is 'So much the better. How the extra quality is put into the "Quality First" Morris'.

The ferry-crossing image (bottom left) is used for the cover of English and foreign-language Minor catalogues dated 1956 and 1957. Also dated 1956 is the catalogue above this, bearing the 'Now BETTER than ever!' slogan. The three 'Together . . . you'll choose' catalogues are a Morris range catalogue for 1959 (yellow), a Minor-only catalogue dated 9/58 (white), and another Minor item dated 1/61 (blue). The Minor catalogues comprise a single 22 x 25³/8 inch sheet, folding to regular 11 x 8¹/2 inch landscape format, while the range catalogue is a single 22 x 8¹/2 inch sheet, side-folded.

This catalogue, with the 'Now BETTER than ever!' coverline (dated 11/56) has all-new artwork and a stapled 16-page format; content emphasises the worldwide appeal of the Minor.

For the 1959 model year the 'Together . . . you'll choose' catalogue introduced a poster-style centre spread of small artwork images.

The early 1961 version of the 'Together . . . you'll choose' catalogue with the blue cover uses essentially the same artwork as found on the white-covered version, but has a different presentation for the left-hand sidebar.

Traveller catalogues from the 'Together . . . you'll choose' era: a treble-folded single-sheet format is used, with a mix of colour artwork and ink sketches against spot colour backgrounds. These two examples, dated 9/59 and 7/60, are identical but for slight differences in colouring.

For 1959 the yellow-covered Morris range catalogue (above), carries the then current advertising slogan 'Together . . . you'll choose a Morris'. The red-covered range catalogue for 1962 emphasises the family appeal of Morris cars.

The range catalogue for 1959 Morrises (upper left) is a single sheet unfolding into a poster-format spread, with colour artwork throughout. The 1962 range catalogue (left) is a four-sider with a side fold and uninspiring mono artwork.

New cover images came in with the 1098cc engine, but inside the Minor catalogue the same basic poster-style spread of artwork was used. The left-hand catalogue is dated 9/62, the right-hand 9/63.

Artwork on the 1962/63 Minor catalogues shows gloveboxes without their lids, and the engine colour is changed from gold to green; also there is a new image showing the paper-element air-cleaner. Some colours change, too.

Chapter Nine

Minors
in miniature

FOR THE BEST-SELLING car from Britain's biggest manufacturer, the Minor was in its day surprisingly neglected by the toy manufacturers.

Die-cast metal models

Of the 'Big Three' makers of die-cast metal toys, only Matchbox offered a Minor; neither Dinky nor Corgi modelled the Morris in their mainstream 1:43 series, although between them the two firms covered most other mass-produced British cars. Admittedly, Dinky produced a Minor mail van in its short-lived small-scale 'Dublo' range, but beyond that it was left to the Belfast-based Tri-ang brand Spot-On to wave the flag for quality metal models of the Minor.

Plastic models

Turn to the medium of plastic, and the picture is better, with a wide range of Minor saloons, and at least one van, being available over the years. First in the field, in November 1948, were the clockwork Minic 1:43 Minors, and these were closely followed by the similar Brimtoy miniatures and by the expensive and well-detailed battery-powered 1:20 Victory models. Various cheap plastic-bodied Minors followed, in either hard or soft plastic.

The trouble, however, is that hard-plastic models tend to be easily destroyed by over-exuberant children, while the large-scale soft-plastic models are too bulky to have been kept in any numbers. Collecting period models of the Minor can thus be quite a challenge, once you've moved beyond the easily sourced Matchbox and expensive but not particularly scarce Spot-On Minor 1000s.

Collector's models

In compensation, since the 1980s the adult market for collector's models and white-metal kits has served the Minor enthusiast well. At the bottom end of the spectrum Corgi and Lledo between them offer moderately priced versions of two-door, convertible, Traveller, van and pick-up Minor 1000s. For those prepared to assemble their own model, white-metal kits in large and small (OO) scales are available for sundry Minor types. Finally, there are various built-up white-metal models, some of these also being available in kit form.

The Corgi and Lledo vans in particular lend themselves to models in period or promotional/commemorative livery, and the issuing of special versions of Corgi and Lledo Minors, mostly vans, has become an epidemic. Corgi above all has sought to milk this market for all it is worth, often with scant regard to authenticity. To collect both Corgi special editions and specially commissioned ('Code 3', as they're called) models based on Corgi and Lledo models is an easy route to bankruptcy.

The missing Minor models

Illustrated in this chapter are almost all known period miniature Minors, most specialist modern models, and a sprinkling of Corgi and Lledo offerings. A notable 1950s/'60s absentee is a 1:30 red plastic Royal Mail van made in Hong Kong by OK. The author has also seen references to a 1:20 plastic late Series II saloon by Tudor Rose, current in the '50s, and to an MM-shaped pencil-sharpener, which is presumed to be a period item.

Current offerings not photographed include the white-metal 1:43 Traveller and van of K&R Replicas, available either as kits or ready-made, and the 1:43 white-metal 'cheesegrater-grille' SII breakdown truck and Morris Motors fire-engine of RAE Models, again available either built-up or as a kit. The fire-engine was also until recently offered as a resin kit by Italian firm Equipe Tron.

Finally, an oddity you may come across is a Minor 1000 pick-up converted from a Corgi van with a 'transkit' conversion pack. These were offered by Model Road & Rail, who also supplied ready-converted vans in the form of either a Job's Dairy pick-up or the Morris Motors fire-engine. The company also briefly produced 'transkits' to make a Convertible out of the Corgi saloon.

The first Minor models were these plastic medium-scale (approximately 1:43) models of the low-light MM manufactured by Tri-ang and Brimtoys. Far left, in green and with a removable alloy key, is the clockwork Tri-ang Minic interpretation; the base is in painted metal. Next to it, in the centre of the photo, is a dark blue Minic without its key. Less hard to find are the Wells Brimtoy MMs. Available in red, blue, silver and green, and either unmotorised or with a clockwork or friction mechanism, there are in all 15 variants. The two pale blue cars to the rear are unmotorised Brimtoys, again plastic-bodied with a metal base, while to the right is a clockwork Brimtoy with trailer. A tinplate car transporter loaded with two Minors was another Brimtoy offering. All the models measure approximately 3³/₈ inches.

Minic MM with clockwork mechanism and removable key. These Minic models, offered in blue, green, red, silver and gold, and with or without a clockwork mechanism, are now quite rare; they were also available with a roof-mounted speaker.

Unmotorised Brimtoy MM.

The other early manufacturer of Minor models was Guildford-based Victory Industries (Surrey) Ltd, which produced its Minors in collaboration with the Nuffield Organisation; boxing represented a Nuffield Exports crate. Large-scale and well-detailed, the 1:20 Victory Minors are 8 inches long – here a 1:42 Spot-On gives scale – and feature a 'Mighty Midget' battery-powered motor.

Initially sold as a 'lowlight', the model was subsequently revised into highlight MM form, then into 1954–56 Series II form, before ultimately being re-moulded as a Minor 1000. This last variant was sold with or without remote control of the steering. Only two-door versions of the Minor were ever offered by Victory; other colours can be found.

The Victory 'Highlight' MM poses with a catalogue depicting an alternative presentation box. The bodies of the Victory Minors are in plastic, with a steel-sheet chassis and a folded-steel seat insert, and with the bumpers, grille surround, grille, bonnet badge and side stripes in aluminium. There is Ackermann-type steering, and the oversize rubber tyres are embossed 'Dunlop Fort'.

The only widely available 'facelift' 1954–56 Series II Minor produced at the time was the Dublo Dinky Royal Mail van. Measuring 1⁷⁄₈ inches, it is to OO railway scale (hence 'Dublo'), equivalent to 1:75, and is in cast metal with windows. The model was available from 1959 until 1964, and was offered alongside a well-executed Cowley 1⁄2-ton (ie MO-based) pick-up.

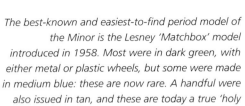

The best-known and easiest-to-find period model of the Minor is the Lesney 'Matchbox' model introduced in 1958. Most were in dark green, with either metal or plastic wheels, but some were made in medium blue: these are now rare. A handful were also issued in tan, and these are today a true 'holy grail' for collectors.

Dating seemingly from the early 1960s, the grey plastic Minor 1000 shown here with its box was made by Lucky. A reasonably accurate representation of a four-door 1000, it is UK-made, in this instance, although some were manufactured in Hong Kong. It measures approximately 7 inches long, and has a front-mounted friction motor.

In front is a crude one-piece moulded-plastic 'lowlight' measuring 2¹⁄₄ inches. Made by 'PML', it was bought new by the author in Zimbabwe (formerly Rhodesia) in 1991. Sold as part of a plastic bag of very 1950s cars and lorries (including an Austin Atlantic and a Hudson), it is probably of Zimbabwean (or possibly South African) manufacture, and may well still be obtainable. Again, a 1:42 Spot-On Minor gives scale.

The sub-OO plastic Minor 1000 (right) you might have found floating in your bowl of Kellogg's cereal during an in-pack giveaway promotion back in the 1950s; the windows have been cut out by the model's then youthful owner. Alongside, to give scale, is the ex-Zimbabwe 'lowlight'.

The only period regular-size die-cast offering was from Tri-ang, whose Spot-On brand offered this well-detailed 1:42 Minor 1000 four-door between 1965 and 1967. Available in pale blue (the most common), red, and metallic green (the most rare), Spot-On Minors command high prices: a mint-and-boxed example is sufficiently sought-after and rare to command up to £150. The plastic chromework is now reproduced.

The Spot-On Minor also served in the 1980s as the basis for DGM's white-metal Series II and 1000 models, offered as both a saloon and a convertible, and for a 1000 saloon on wide wheels made by the Australian firm Bonza. Currently SLMC ('Steve's Little Motor Company') offers white-metal 1000 four-door kits moulded from the Spot-On shell.

This delightful 1960s plastic 1:36 kit of a Minor 1000 Traveller is in Revell's 'Cadet' series and is extremely rare – unsurprisingly, as most would have been made up by children and then duly destroyed. Excellently detailed, it features silver-plastic brightwork and a build-it-yourself four-part body shell. It represents a Minor with 'clap-hands' wipers, and the instructions refer to a 948cc engine.

A typical crude soft-plastic toy of the 1950s (perhaps even the early '60s) is the red late Series II two-door on the left. British-made, and approximately 7³/4 inches long, it is adequately accurate and features press-in combined wheels and axles in silver plastic; it seems to have been moulded off the Victory model. It was sold as a container for an Easter egg, and was also available in orange and blue. Beside it is a yellow squashy-plastic baby's toy dating probably from the 1980s. The squeaky rubber red Minor alongside is thought to be of the same era.

Mikansue (Mike and Sue Richardson) was one of the earliest British companies to produce white-metal 1:43 kits. This Minor 1000 Traveller was purchased in 1980, at which time the firm was also offering, among other things, a 'lowlight MM', a Mosquito, a van, and a pick-up – as well as a very reasonable Morris Eight Series E four-door saloon. Plastic tyres and chromed brightwork feature, and accuracy is generally acceptable. Mikansue models were current from the late 1970s until the end of the '80s.

Since the 1980s Springside Models has been offering the entire Minor 1000 range, including the van and pick-up, in build-it-yourself white-metal OO scale; the models are intended for display with OO-scale railways. The Convertible kit shown has 18 parts (including a choice of raised or lowered hood), plus six microscopic jewelled lights. Built up, it measures 2 inches long.

Rather simpler OO-scale models are these from Scale Link (left) and Midget Models (right). The Scale Link offering is a late SII Traveller, while the Midget Models Minor is a 1000 four-door, seemingly modelled off the 'Matchbox' die-cast and suffering from a slightly squashed-down body. Behind is another white-metal 1000 saloon, of unknown origin. As well as the SII Traveller, W&T Manufacturing, which has taken over Scale Link, now offers a late SII pick-up and a late SII van (with or without Royal Mail transfers), and is working on Minor 1000 saloon and Convertible models.

These three 1:43 scale Minor 1000 two-door saloons are by Period Models, and were sold as fully-made-up collector's white-metal models. Four colours were offered, and the total production run was only 500 units.

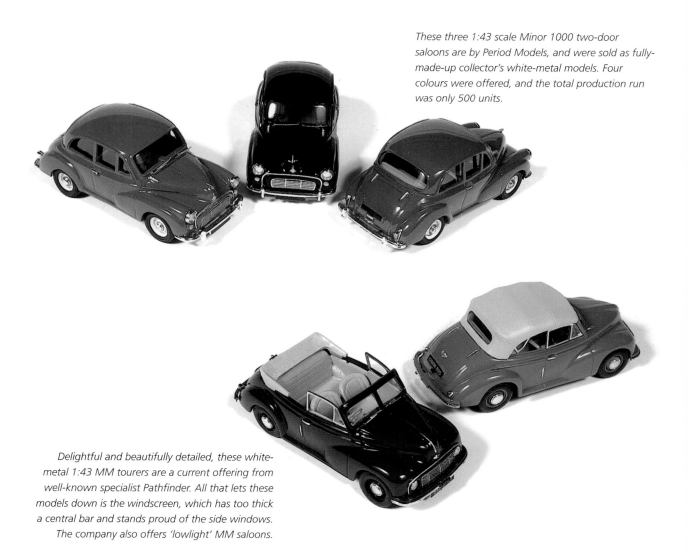

Delightful and beautifully detailed, these white-metal 1:43 MM tourers are a current offering from well-known specialist Pathfinder. All that lets these models down is the windscreen, which has too thick a central bar and stands proud of the side windows. The company also offers 'lowlight' MM saloons.

Brass and pewter ornamental models became very popular in the 1990s. The small pewter Minor 1000 two-door is a little bit on the narrow side. The 1954–56 two-door Series II appears to be cast from an adaptation of the Corgi Minor 1000 casting, while the 1000 van would seem to be based on the Corgi van.

This Minor teapot is one of the many ceramic Minor items available, ranging from toothbrush holders to salt-and-pepper sets and table lamps.

Although available at swapmeets and autojumbles and high street shops for as little as £1, these Chinese-made 'Golden Wheel' two-door saloons (length just over 4 inches) are actually a very good casting. Slightly larger than the Corgi Minor, at approximately 1:30, they have good interior detail and are only marred by the inaccurate and sharp-angled plastic radiator grille and surround. Black, green, blue and pink versions are available, and an oddball adaptation is a New York cab version on sale in the States. The shell is currently being adapted by DGM (Dave Gilbert Models) as the basis for a new moulding, which will be enhanced by reshaped brightwork in metal.

Corgi now offers Minor 1000s in two-door, convertible, van, Traveller and pick-up versions; the first to appear, in 1988, was the two-door. All are unimpressive in their detailing – the convertible less so – and all suffer from over-glossy paint. Countless different versions have been produced over the years, to milk the lucrative collectors' market; shown here are a Police panda-car, a bomb-disposal Traveller (with plastic accessories), and a reproduction of the former Morris Motors factory fire engine. The last still exists, and was in fact an experimental late 1951 'highlight' MM chassis/cab unit, with the doors welded up and then deeply cut away. Corgi has been content, however, merely to offer a repaint of its Minor 1000 pick-up casting.

The continual issuing of Corgi promotional vans, either by Corgi itself or by specialist firms, has reached epidemic proportions. Four typical examples are shown: a Morris Minor Owners' Club promo for the 1992 national rally at Billing, a Hull Daily Mail van from 1989 (a 1,000-off limited edition to celebrate the Mail's move to new offices), a promo for the MMOC, and finally a police van produced by Gerry Ford Design of Farnborough. This last is typical of how a specialist modeller can enhance the basic model. In comparison with Corgi's own police van, it has finer decals, and is fully equipped with a searchlight, horns, a roof light, and two – instead of one – 'Police' roof signs.

Corgi's China-made Minor 1000 convertible is available with the roof either up or down. More finely detailed than the saloon both outside and inside, it has chromed-plastic windscreen wipers, door handles and wing mirrors; various colours are available.

These limited editions by Corgi celebrate the Colin Moles London-to-Peking fundraising car (left), the Rupert Jones/Philip Young Himalayan Rally Minor (centre, on plinth), and (right) the Pat Moss rally car 'Granny'. In front is a limited edition Himalayan Rally Minor by a small specialist firm: note how the decals are crisper and more accurate.

This plated Minor from Corgi's 'Connoisseur Collection' is one of only 1,000 produced in a special 1993 issue, and retailed at £35. The car is mounted on a black plastic plinth and has a black board box.

Both Lledo and Corgi offer Minor 1000 vans; the Lledo, on the right, is clearly a better effort, with a more accurate shape to the rear windows and a more realistic track. As with all Lledo models, it is made in Great Britain. In comparison, the Corgi has sides that are too flat, raised sections in the rear doors that are too long, and door windows of incorrect shape.

A comparison between Lledo (front) and Corgi Minor 1000 Travellers. The Corgi version, made in China, has a particularly ham-fisted grille treatment, and that on the Lledo isn't quite right either. The Lledo is a 'second generation' example, with grey plastic wheels, a chromed grille, and a silver-painted coachline (wrongly placed) on the doors; the first Lledo Travellers had cream plastic wheels and grille, and no coachline.

The current Lledo Traveller, in a series now called 'Vanguards', features chromed hubcaps, a correctly positioned coachline, and a reversion to a cream plastic grille. Also the grille outer surround, hinges, badges and lights are picked out in paint, and wiper arms have been added to the casting. Lledo Minor vans have followed the same evolution, and are now a very effective model.

The Minor in Corgi's small-scale 'Sixties Cameo Collection' has appeared in various guises: as mainstream Corgi 'Cameo', as Fina and Kelloggs promotional giveaways (with the other models in the series), and as part of a 1993 Cadbury's boxed set with other cars in the series. The Fina Minor, incidentally, seems only to have been available in lilac, a colour not offered for Minors in regular 'Cameo' boxing. Despite supposedly being a '60s collection, the Minor is a 1954–56 Series II – while the VW is a 1953–57 car with oval rear screen, and the 2CV is a 1957–61 model; the final car in the series is a 1959–67 Mk I Mini.

Chapter Ten

Twin-cam conversions

PUTTING FIAT twin-cam engines in Morris Minors is hardly going to win you Brownie points with the purist brigade. But if you want a Minor that will see off MGBs without even trying – and won't break the bank – then it's a conversion worth investigating.

The leading exponents of this engine swap are brothers Robin and John Beardmore. Between them, as a private venture, they turn out twin-cam Minors that are fully sorted and professionally engineered, with the running gear as carefully executed as their engine installations. And having driven a trio of their conversions – and driven them hard – the author can vouch for their effectiveness: they're fun with a capital 'F', with none of the rough edges you might expect from cars put together on a tight budget in an ordinary domestic single garage.

Robin and John have now carried out over ten conversions, beginning when John was 17 years old. That first car took nine weeks to convert; now the brothers – today both qualified engineers – can do the job in three to four days.

More bang for fewer bucks

But why put a Fiat twin-cam in a Minor? For John, who has a degree in Manufacturing Systems Engineering, it was the logical way to give his Minor a strong, durable power unit on the cheap, back in 1986.

'I used to run a tuned Midget engine, but I blew that up. The choice was either another Midget engine or the Fiat conversion, which I'd read about in *Street Machine*. But using the Minor in local road rallies, the Midget gearboxes kept breaking, and the drive-train couldn't really cope with the power. With the Fiat, £150–200 will bring you a reliable 115bhp, a twin-cam engine, and a matching five-speed gearbox.'

Over the years, the brothers have improved the transplant process, as they've gone through their training as engineers and have previously developed a greater appreciation of the engineering principles involved.

'We've refined the installation in areas such as the choice of radiator, fan and hoses, and things such as the throttle linkage, so it'll look more like a professional conversion,' says Robin, currently a production engineer at the Vickers tank factory.

Not only that, but John has now given a British twist to the operation by devising a manifold to take twin SU carburetters. Compared to the Fiat engine's single Weber, these give better drivability, more performance, and are easier to tune.

Finding an engine

These days the donor car will be a 131/Mirafiori or a 132/Argenta, and that means a choice of 1600cc, 1800cc

A major achievement: John Beardmore's moulds for casting a manifold to take twin SUs – and the end result. These guys aren't casual weekend tinkerers. (John Beardmore)

or 2000cc power units, almost invariably with a five-speed box. If you use a late 132 or Argenta engine, from a car with power-assisted steering, you'll have to swap the larger front pulley for a 131 item or else cut it down to remove the power-steering drive pulley. With supplies of 131s drying up, it's worth knowing that you can also use the transverse engine from the Fiat Regata, Fiat Croma or Lancia Beta, but then you'll need to sort out an appropriate gearbox.

Engine installation

The engine installation is basically straightforward, thanks to the generous size of the Minor engine bay and such helpful design features as bolt-in engine mounts, a flat engine compartment floor, and front panelwork that completely unbolts.

All the same, it's a tight fit, and one that's only made possible by omitting the inner front panel on which the radiator is normally mounted. It is also necessary to cut a section from the Fiat bellhousing, to allow clearance for the Minor's high-mounted steering rack.

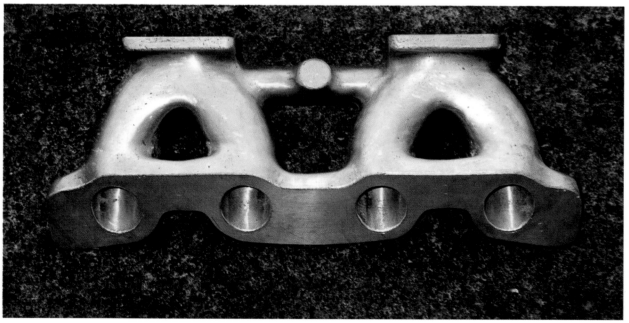

The Fiat bellhousing needs to be carefully cut to allow clearance for the Minor rack. An exposed clutch is not a problem. (John Beardmore)

in a square-tube crossmember.

'Now we just trim back the original chassis member and re-box it,' says John. 'It's much stronger than the original method, which we used because we thought it was necessary if we wanted to get the engine in and out easily.'

Engine mounts are Beardmore-fabricated, from plate, and take standard Fiat or Lada rubbers. The rubbers are angled to help counteract engine vibration; this arrangement duplicates the original Fiat method and has superseded the earlier Beardmore system of box-section mounts with vertical rubbers.

The final element is a new gearbox-mounting crossmember to replace the Minor's bolt-in folded-steel cradle. Originally Robin and John used a square-tube crosspiece attached rigidly to the gearbox but flexibly mounted to brackets on the chassis rails via cut-down Minor gearbox rubbers.

'The problem is that the Minor cross-member is solidly bolted between the chassis rails and adds a degree of strength to the structure,' says John. 'We were taking this out. So what we do now is bolt in our new crossmember solidly, and use a rubber mounting for the gearbox – with a Cortina rubber in a fabricated bracket.'

For the oil filter to clear the chassis a Mirafiori 1600 filter housing can be used, with a smaller-than-normal filter; even then you have to remove the filter complete with the housing at oil-change time. A better solution is to fit a Regata filter housing, which points horizontally backwards. A remote oil filter is another possibility, as is fitting an inverter block to turn the filter assembly on its head. This last approach John doesn't like, as it leads to a drop in oil pressure. Finally, for hard driving an oil cooler doesn't go amiss, and the Beardmores use a proprietary Mocal unit mounted at the back of the engine bay and fed air via a duct from the grille.

Care should be taken here to achieve smooth radii to the corners, thus limiting the risk of cracks developing; the aperture should ideally then have a dirt-excluding plate Araldited in place, if space allows. The Minor's removable gearbox cover will also have to be cut-and-shut to fit over the Fiat box.

The only metal-cutting required on the Minor body is at the front of the engine bay. Originally the Beardmores chopped out the box section running across the front of the bay and linking the two chassis legs, in its place bolting

Remodelling the screw-in transmission cover is a minor task, relative to the rest of the installation. (John Beardmore)

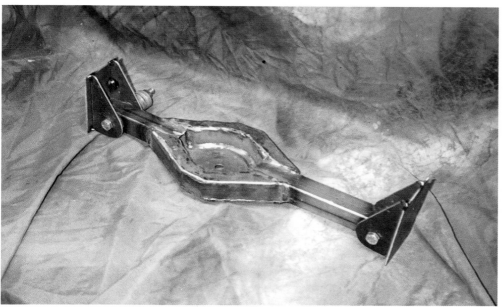

The Beardmore rear crossmember. The carriers at each end are welded to the chassis rails – a good solid installation results. (John Beardmore)

Clutch modifications

Clutch actuation changes from the Minor's rod-operated system to the Fiat's cable set-up. Robin and John cut off the actuating arm from the Minor pedal, weld on a longer arm, and fabricate a cable mounting bracket, which bolts in place via the captive nuts previously used to secure the Minor's clutch relay shaft.

Cooling system

Moving on to the cooling system, the Beardmores have ditched the marginal Allegro radiator they used to fit, and now use a Marina item re-cored to

Sherpa diesel specification. This is carried out by a local radiator specialist who also fits Cortina outlet stubs. Hoses are trimmed-down Sierra ohc, a BMC A-series thermostat is used under

the outlet in the top of the Fiat's head, and either a proprietary Pacet or Clova electric fan or a modified Nissan Cherry unit is winkled in – and that's the operative word, as one of the grille slats has to be cut away to make room for it.

Making your own twin-cam Minor

The Beardmore cars are purely a private venture. London-based Minor Mania, however, does offer a kit at a price of £350 including VAT, while in Yorkshire a similar but slightly cheaper kit is available from Mighty Minor. These are installation kits only. You'll have to find your own engine and gearbox, and here the sensible advice is to buy a complete running car, so you can assess the state of the power unit and the box before taking the plunge.

The Minor Mania kit comprises front and rear crossmembers, engine mounts, a clutch pedal extension and clutch cable bracket, and a stainless steel large-diameter tubular exhaust manifold. Also included is a bracket to allow use of a supposedly superior Lucas alternator where the Beardmores retain the Fiat unit, and a choice of either a remote installation or an inverter block for the oil filter.

The kit differs in several ways from the Beardmore set-up. The front crossmember is a hefty 2^3/4-inch square-tube bolt-on, for starters. 'It's a lot stronger than the original, which is just two bits of sheet metal,' says Minor Mania's Nick Spanakis.

As for the rear crossmember, this is a steel box structure that bolts *under* the chassis rails rather than flush with them. This cuts down ground clearance, and the Beardmores feel that their solution is better. Finally, the engine mounts are inclined – a good idea, all parties agree.

Minor Mania stocks a range of parts for uprating Minor running gear – from nylon suspension bushes and rose-jointed track-rod ends through to uprated torsion bars and front disc conversions. Spanakis recommends all these, plus a front anti-roll bar, if you're fitting a twin-cam, and he advises telescopic dampers all round as a matter of course.

Other installation suggestions are a Metro turbo radiator and an Escort Mk I/II rear axle. Whether or not to fit a servo comes down to personal taste, says Spanakis.

Up in Castleford, West Yorkshire, Stuart Holmes of Mighty Minor has improved on the Minor Mania kit by designing his own rear crossmember, which gives better ground clearance and is claimed to be easier to fit.

'The conversion is common sense, really,' says Stuart, who also offers suspension mods and his own front disc kit. 'But remember it's your life on the line. Safety is the main thing. If you don't feel competent, leave it alone and get a specialist to do the job for you.'

Final installation details

These include adopting the Fiat propshaft to whatever back axle is used, of which more anon; in fact the brothers now strongly favour a split propshaft, and fabricate a suitable centre support bearing. Then there's a Beardmore-made tubular exhaust manifold, slotting through the appropriate bulkhead aperture without the need for any cutting, and an exhaust system made up from purpose-made bends and new boxes.

Chassis and braking

Chassis and braking naturally have to be uprated, and it goes without saying that the basis for the conversion has to be a structurally sound shell, with all rust cut out and correctly replaced with new metal. There are now quite a few firms offering equipment for modernising the Minor's suspension and braking systems, and the Beardmores have drawn on these while at the same time developing solutions of their own.

But let's not jump ahead of ourselves. Before sorting the chassis it is necessary to make sure that the Fiat engine's power actually makes it to the rear wheels. Stick with a Minor back axle and it'll probably blow itself to bits before you can say 'Alec Issigonis'.

Robin and John favour the Toyota Celica Mk I or Mk II back axle. The width is correct, and in GT form it'll have a limited-slip diff, yet you can pick one up for £30 or less – when a new LSD could set you back £200–300; it also has the correct stud spacing to take 14-inch Austin A60 wheels, which look like standard Minor rims and take Minor hubcaps. Other possibilities are a

Ford Escort Mk I/II (allowing a good choice of wheels and of axle ratios), a Dolomite/Marina unit, or an A60 axle if you want to stay BMC and 'period'.

Handbrake linkages and spring mountings will need to be sorted out, then there's the question of tying the axle down. The comprehensive suspension packages offered by Chris Street and by Charles Ware's Morris Minor Centre tackle this extremely effectively by using turreted telescopic dampers mounted on the inner wing, in conjunction with radius arms; this arrangement does, however, limit the width of wheel that can be accommodated. The bolt-on Spax telescopic conversion is another – simpler – possibility.

The Beardmores do it differently: primarily out of the need to allow wheel-arch clearance for wide tyres, they opt for inboard turreted telescopics, mounted in the boot. Experiments with Volvo radius arms weren't a success, so this is as far as the brothers go.

At the front Robin and John have generally used either the Spax telescopic conversion or Chris Street's installation, which they regard as the most professional on the market; John is now moving, however, to a conversion of his own making. On the question of anti-roll bars, the brothers are sceptics: none of their cars has used them.

Front discs are a 'given', with the widespread acceptance these days of converting Minors to take Marina discs; Robin and John use the kit offered by Minor uprater Owen Burton. Normally such a move entails either using Marina wheels or else machining the hubs to take studs spaced for Minor wheels, if you want your car to look 'stock'. However, if you use Marina 575 van or pick-up hubs, the stud spacing allows you to use those A60 wheels, which also fit the Celica back axle . . .

If you fit discs, the received wisdom is that you then fit a remote reservoir, because of the Minor master cylinder's small capacity, and you install a servo.

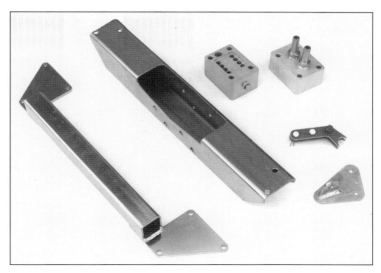

The essential components of the Minor Mania kit: front crossmember (foreground), rear crossmember, oil filter adapter blocks, clutch pedal extension, and clutch cable bracket. (Author)

In fact the Beardmores have never fitted an extra reservoir, and find that they rarely need to top up the master cylinder. Nor is John convinced about servos:

'Our philosophy is to keep things simple. So there's no servo – it's extra cost, and it's something else to go wrong. Without one, you have a solid pedal, but at least you know where you are with it.'

Andrew Booth's 2-litre saloon

Registered nurse Andrew Booth had the Beardmores convert his 1958 Minor back in 1988, using £150 of 2-litre Fiat 132 hardware and for an all-in cost of £500. Since then he's covered an average of 5,000 miles a year, with impressive reliability.

'When we'd installed the engine, we took the head off, and we gave it a full service. It started first time, and it's run well ever since, with just routine servicing. The only problems have been an electrical fault and various exhaust failures – the exhaust has proved the weakest link, and it's constantly blowing. It's otherwise proved very reliable over the years, which is pretty incredible for a 40-year-old car.'

Andrew has departed from the 132's standard single Weber twin-choke, fit-

A bonnet full of twin-cam: Andrew Booth's car runs twin Webers, not something that in retrospect he'd recommend. This is one of the Beardmores' earliest conversions. (James Mann/Classic and Sports Car)

The joy of a twin-cam conversion is that it needn't shout out. Andrew Booth's grey four-door could be just any district nurse's runabout. But just watch jaws drop as it takes out Vectra-driving reps! (James Mann/Classic and Sports Car)

ting a pair of 40 DCOEs on a Mangoletsi manifold:

'This set-up is very temperamental, and I don't recommend it. The carbs make the fuel consumption worse, they're a hassle to fit, and the car's a lot noisier – the intake roar can sometimes be deafening.

'But at the Morris Minor Owners' Club custom register's 1990 Santa Pod meet I clocked 16.04 seconds for the standing quarter-mile – the fastest time for a 2-litre Minor. You'd have to spend a lot more to get the same performance with an A-series engine . . .'

And performance you certainly get: giving Andrew's car its head on the motorway saw the needle 80mph speedo off the clock and right round the fuel gauge. That translates into a stable and undramatic 90mph, and still going strong – plus a few surprised sales reps in their Vectras.

Rick Beardmore's 2-litre convertible

The 2-litre convertible of Rick Beardmore, father of Robin and John, convinces even more. Looking refreshingly standard, this converted saloon has a stock 132 engine and various special features. These include false sides to the engine bay to hide the wiring and give an ultra-clean look, a 10-gallon Fiat fuel tank, and extra-long turreted rear dampers. A retired telephone engineer, Rick uses the car to tow his caravan on overseas trips and as a fun second car.

It's some machine. The Fiat engine gives the Minor the muscular performance you'd expect, with buckets of mid-range torque, effortless acceleration, and relaxed 80–90mph cruising. There's decent refinement, too, owing to a transversely mounted Volvo exhaust (made possible by the Fiat tank) and the standard tune of the engine – which the Beardmores generally favour. The five-speed change, actuated by a pleasant stubby lever, is fast and unobstructive, and in common with

Immaculate presentation of the car built for father Rick Beardmore. The 'smooth-look' panelled-in sides and bulkhead conceal the car's wiring. The engine is a 2-litre unit. (James Mann/Classic and Sports Car)

The Rick Beardmore car in build: the spaciousness of the Minor engine bay is a big help. The cut-away and re-shaped front panel is stronger than a bolt-in member and is now the brothers' preferred way of doing things. The engine mounts sitting flat on the side panels have been replaced by angled mounts in the latest Beardmore conversions. (John Beardmore)

Andrew's car the firm clutch has none of the judder one might expect of a home-brewed installation.

What's so impressive, though, is how the easy power of the Fiat engine is so readily useable, thanks to the competence of the chassis. The brakes, for starters, are excellent: with a firm

short-travel action and plenty of bite, they haul the car down swiftly and four-square. Without a servo, they feel a tad wooden, and you do have to lean on the pedal for rapid stops, but their effectiveness is never in doubt, and the pedal feel is nicely in harmony with that of the clutch.

The suspension is tied down sufficiently to give a ride that's firm but rubbery rather than harsh, with well-controlled damping. Helped by the beautifully quick and informative Minor rack, handling is as nimble as ever, the extra weight of the engine having no noticeable effect on the safely neutral cornering stance with which standard Minors are blessed. Nor does the car roll to any degree, despite the absence of a front anti-roll bar.

Nigel Morris's 1600 convertible

Accountant Nigel Morris's mildly customised tourer was built by the Beardmores around a van chassis, and thus is much more rigid than the normal article. Leaving aside its tauter structure, and the go-kart handling imparted by the lowered suspension and low-profile 185x50/14 rubber, where Nigel's car scores is in the sweetness of its 1600 engine.

Smoother and more free-revving, it still turns in a strong performance: at 70mph in fifth it's doing 3750rpm and there's power in hand to surge past slower cars. This is a standard single-carb engine, hauled from a scrap 131, but it sure delivers, helped by a longer-throw non-remote gearchange that has a metallic directness and never misses a slot.

Drive Rick's car and Nigel's back to back and the appeal of these twin-cam Minors comes through loud and clear. Strong performance from a technically interesting engine with a Ferrari heritage is only part of the story. So is the low cost — say £1,000 all-in — of obtaining such unstressed and delightfully delivered power. What really makes the package so seductive is the essential straightforwardness of the conversion, and the way in which the rest of the car can be so effectively honed to make a totally useable high-speed Q-car. The coming together of Turin and Cowley might seem a strange marriage, but for broad-minded Minor fans it's a match made in heaven.

Chapter Eleven

Minor miscellany

• The 'lowlight' configuration of the original MM wasn't just a stylistic solution. The lamps were mounted so that the orthodox headlamp bowl could be dispensed with – and at the same time the lamps could provide under-bonnet illumination.

• The Minor in its heyday was a valued moneyspinner for Nuffield and BMC. 'The company made about £40 per car, which was a handsome profit,' recalls Gerald Palmer. 'It really built up Nuffield's finances.' Former Nuffield accountant Mark Yeatman-Reed says that the original profit for the MM was £13 8s 4d per vehicle – a different figure, but still a pretty respectable one when at its launch the MM saloon was selling at £358 10s 7d.

• The Minor was originally to have had the fuel tank incorporated in the floor pressing, with a lid welded to the top – and thereby hangs a fascinating story. The idea was abandoned, and in its place Morris Radiators Branch devised a drop-in tank made of two pressings with flanges, these being continuously welded together with a wheel-welder. When it came to devising the construction for the Mini's body, this process was borrowed, and the Mini shell was wheel-welded around exposed seams. The result, says Jack Daniels, was a body well over 10 per cent stronger than if spot-welding had been used. All thanks to the Minor fuel tank . . .

• It was intended to fit the Minor with a steering-column gearchange at the same time as the Wolseley Eight engine. With the arrival of the Austin A30 engine and gearbox this never happened, of course, but the front-wheel-drive Minor was given a column change – for reasons of engineering convenience.

This Morris Minor motorvan is called 'The Snail' and features a Fisher Holivan caravan mounted back-to-front on a Minor van chassis; the fearsome rear overhang must make for interesting handling. Rostyle wheels were fitted after the previous rear wheels fractured under the strain . . . (Author)

This 1950s-style custom Series II, photographed in the '80s, features rear spats and a recessed spare wheel. (Author)

A Minor four-door converted into a 'woody' using the back end of a Traveller, including the rear wings. (Minor Matters)

Another motorvan, this time one built by Jim Lambert, who makes the reduced-scale children's Minor seen in the foreground. (Author)

Two pick-ups made from Travellers: neither is exactly elegant. (Minor Matters)

- The Minor was intended to be produced at roughly twice the rate of the bigger Oxford: in 1950 the maximum weekly output attainable at Cowley was given as 1,356 Minors (excluding commercials) and 728 Oxfords, out of a total capacity of 3,228 cars per week. This ratio was largely achieved: a total of 305,203 Minors were made between 1948 and 1954, and a rather less substantial 159,960 MO-series Oxfords.

- British-assembled versions of the Citroën 2CV, made in Slough between 1953 and 1959, used a Morris Minor rear bumper valance as a front bumper, with cut-down Minor over-riders.

- The custom fraternity has grafted various noses on to the Minor. One car has an Austin A40 Devon front, several have replica 1940s Willys fronts in glass-fibre, and in Australia there's a Minor adapted to take the front grille from a Morris Nomad. If you don't know what that is, it's a BMC 1100/1300 with a Maxi 1500 engine and a hatchback rear. Honest.

- Minors were assembled in South Africa, and were a popular choice for local motor sport. One stripped-out split-screen ran a three-cylinder two-stroke DKW engine. Another Minor, used in club racing, had a 1500cc Borgward Isabella engine.

- Most unlikely Morris Minor driver? Raw acid-etched junkie rock legend Janis Joplin, better known automotively for her psychedelic-painted Porsche 356. In 1961, as an 18-year-old fresh from dropping out of college in Texas, Joplin escaped to Los Angeles for the summer in a Minor convertible, which, according to biographer Ellis Amburn, 'she'd picked up somewhere along the line'.

  Closer to home, stylishly cool singer and former Roxy Music frontman Bryan Ferry used to own a Minor Traveller, bought off his old friend Charlie Ware. 'I have always considered the Morris Minor to be a classic car, and driving one was a lot of fun,' Ferry told the author. Another rock-world Minor man is Tom Robinson, of 'Glad to be Gay' and '2-4-6-8 Motorway' fame.

  Others in the public eye to have owned Minors include Stirling Moss, fellow racing driver Roy Salvadori, former Governor of Hong Kong Chris Patten, impersonator Faith Brown, racer and TV personality Tiff Needell, and furniture-maker Lord Linley.

The infamous 'Morrari', photographed at Pukekohe, New Zealand, in the mid-1960s. Underneath the 'lowlight' bodyshell is the chassis of a 1955 Ferrari Tipo 555 'Supersqualo' Grand Prix car and a Chevrolet Corvette V8. The 'Morrari' was painted bright orange and was driven by top stock-car driver Garth Souness. Straight-line performance was as eye-wateringly quick as you'd expect, but the short wheelbase made the car twitchy on corners. (David Gerrard)

This boot conversion in glass-fibre was offered in 1955 by the Alexander Engineering Co, at a price of £12 10s. At least one example survives. (Autocar)

One of the cleverest recent custom Minors is Gary Bezer's chopped Series II Traveller, powered by a Rover V8. Re-making the timber for the roof-chop was no picnic. Presentation is immaculate. (Author)

A rather woodier 'woody': this modified late Traveller has timber infill between the main ash frame members. (Rob Robinson)

Imaginative engineering has gone into this custom Minor, which features a flip front, a square-tube front subframe and coil-spring front suspension. Power comes from a 2-litre Vauxhall twin-cam. (Author)

London specialist Minor Mania uses this smart six-wheel pick-up. (Author)

Possibly the only surviving Danish-built Minor De Luxe van, marketed by Danish Morris importer DOMI. Apparently these were offered in both Series II and 1000 form, but it is thought that only 50 or so were made. The body is in steel, longer than that of a normal Minor van, and has a roof infill panel; a side-opening rear door is a distinctive feature. The bullet-hole roof vents are not standard. (Anton Kamp Nielsen)

The Jarvis conversion (left) with a standard Morris tourer, showing the changed appearance of the quarters. The coupé hood mohair material sets smoothly when erected.

Tourer to Coupé
HOOD CONVERSION FOR THE MORRIS MINOR

DESIGNED to cross the subtle dividing line between an open tourer and a drop-head coupé, the hood the sidescreen conversion shown in the photographs is being done by Jarvis and Sons, Ltd., the well-known Nuffield distributors, of Morris House, Morden Road, London, S.W.19. The increase of price over the standard tourer is £21 and the conversion itself is not subject to purchase tax.

The material used is a lined mohair to match the car's colour, and the resultant hood has a clean and firm line. Some window space is sacrificed in the quarters,

but it is possible to leave the side screens of the conversion erected when the hood is down. The thicker hood material is an aid to silence of the body.

It is claimed that provision for fixing the side screens and the rear of the hood on the inside of the body makes the car as thief-proof as possible, and the ensemble is rounded off by a matching tonneau cover. The customer may retain the old hood and cover if he wishes.

The conversion usually takes three or four days after the delivery of the mohair hood material, which is at present taking about a week.

The top folds neatly and has a cover.

Something Like Leather : UPHOLSTERY MATERIALS WHICH

Wimbledon Nuffield distributors Jarvis & Sons Ltd used to offer their own bodies pre-war, on chassis such as the M-type MG Midget. In 1949 they announced a drophead coupé adaptation of the Minor Tourer, the conversion costing £21. All it consisted of was a re-profiled hood, in lined mohair and with a smaller back window, and a pair of smaller rear sidescreens. The conversion was still available in 1951. (Autocar)

The 'ant-eater' front on A. Barton's racing Minor would appear to use a 'lowlight' front panel and wings – proof that the original Minor front is better aerodynamically. The car was photographed at the May 1963 BRSCC meeting at Mallory Park, where it came in second in the 851cc–1200cc class in the saloon-car race. (Autosport)

- A perhaps unexpected Minor enthusiast was W. O. Bentley, creator of the Bentley motor car, who owned a succession of Minors. In his 1961 autobiography *The Cars in my Life*, Bentley describes the Morris as 'a useful, sensible and thoroughly practical motor car for British roads today'. This was not without qualifications, however. He went on to say, 'I remember telling the Chief Engineer at Nuffield's some years ago that Issigonis had produced the near-perfect small car for British roads . . . but that he should have taken the plunge and insisted on independent suspension at the rear as well as at the front.' Bentley was a pioneer in the use of independent rear suspension in Britain, featuring it on the Lagonda he announced in 1945, so he was naturally a little evangelical about irs.

  As an intriguing footnote, W. O. Bentley at one stage designed, and had produced, a small air-cooled flat-four engine. According to his autobiography it was at that time 'still running quite happily in a Morris Minor somewhere'. Hands up anyone who knows more . . .

- Still on a horizontally opposed kick, how about a quad-cam flat-four Morris Minor? No, really — it did happen. Back in 1957 racing's Formula 2 rules required a $1^1/_2$-litre engine built around a production block. Racing-car builder Paul Emery somewhat ill-advisedly decided to use the flat-four Jowett Javelin/Jupiter engine as the basis for just such an engine. Two dohc heads with 'hemi' combustion chambers were made up, and with the planned fuel injection 150bhp was envisaged. On the carbs initially fitted, 100bhp was delivered in bench tests, and the engine was fitted in a Minor for trials. The crankcase on the notoriously frail Jowett engine split — reportedly three times — and the project was abandoned. The heads survive in Brisbane, Australia. Nor is that the only Jowett-engined Minor: in Rhodesia, as it was then, there was a racing Minor running about in the '60s with the Javelin flat-four under the bonnet.

- Minor convertible owners in the early 1950s who felt that they were losing the battle against the British weather could convert their cars to closed form by buying hard-tops from Turf Motors of Frizinghall, Bradford. Announced in 1952, the top cost £75 including Purchase Tax. It was made in aluminium, over an ash frame, and was covered in black leathercloth. How many were made is not known. Also in 1952, Airflow Streamlines of Northamptonshire offered a similar top, looking uncannily like a regular Minor roof. Again in aluminium, it cost £10 more than the Turf Motors item.

This wild six-wheeler pick-up hides a mid-mounted V8 under the tilt-up bed. (Lucy Brown)

Evidently inspired by the Ford five-window coupé, this radical cut-down four-door has a one-piece steel flip front and a Ford V8. (Lucy Brown)

Just the right nose-down attitude for this chopped stepside, photographed at York Raceway dragstrip. (Lucy Brown)

The long-wheelbase saloon seen in the 1997 film The Borrowers, photographed during its construction. (Lucy Brown)

Power is doubtless more than adequate in the case of this chopped van, which runs a blown 302 ci Ford V8 and was photographed before completion. (Lucy Brown)

- Swiss Morris agent Keller of Zurich came up with a Minor drophead, with wind-down rear windows and a lowline hood. The car was known as the 'Schweizer [Swiss] Cabriolet De Luxe'.

  Still in Switzerland, one enterprising early-'50s owner of a Minor tourer converted his car — one with removable rear sidescreens — into a multi-format vehicle. First he cut away the front-door window frames, to allow a fully open configuration, modifying the frames so that when required they could be secured in place with two screws. Then he modified the hood with two zips, so that the centre section could be furled back in the continental cabriolet-saloon fashion. Finally, for winter conditions he adapted an entire Minor saloon roof, with rear side windows, so it could be used as a hard-top, secured at three points.

- Australians faced with Morris not importing the Minor Traveller came up with their own solution in 1957/58: a Minor pick-up converted into a wood-framed estate. The work of Sydney-based Nuffield distributors Vaughan & Lane, it retained the pick-up's side panels and tailboard, the latter mating to a top-hinged timber-framed tailgate.

- Over 20,000 Minors were made at the MG factory at Abingdon during the years 1960–64 — 10,818 Travellers, 9,147 vans, and 49 pick-ups. 'We judged the relative cost of stitching the things together against those produced at Cowley. The figures were shoved under the carpet very sharply, because they showed Cowley up in a very bad light,' the late former MG boss John Thornley told the author in 1989. 'What was more interesting still was that we hadn't been doing it long before the distributors were saying, "Yes, I'll have five more Travellers, but I want them to be from Abingdon" . . .'

This miserable US offering dated 9/59 is a single mono sheet with a banal photo on one side and specifications on the reverse.

This United States catalogue dated 2/60 has a colour cover and opens to crisp mono photos. Note the whitewalls on the 'Station Wagon'. Unimaginative copywriters still describe the Minor engine as 'husky'.

English and Dutch versions of the Minor catalogue that lasted into the Leyland era – the dates here are 8/66 and 2/69, the later printing carrying the Leyland emblem on the back cover. Dated artwork style and images unchanged from the 1950s show how little BMC/BL cared about presenting the Minor in the most favourable light. With a single sheet only unfolding once, size is also down by a third.

This Leyland-era Danish catalogue is a two-pager with a gatefold across the bottom. It features the 'Morris 1000 Super' in 'Stationcar' and 'Combi' guises. The former is a renamed Traveller, but the 'Combi' is a tax-dodging van version with covered side windows.

Six Morris range catalogues from the late BMC and early BL period. The slender upright-format 5³⁄₈ x 8¹⁄₂ inch offering for the 1963 model year (dated 10/62), left front, is a single sheet with two flaps opening out from the centre; it uses mono images against a black and yellow background. The centre-front landscape-format catalogue is a single sheet unfolding to 22 x 16¹⁄₂ inches. Dated 9/66, it features mono photos with impressionistic sketches; orange spot colour enlivens the presentation. Similar presentation, only with blue spot colour and the disappearance of the sketches, characterises the 1968 model year (9/67 dated) portrait-format catalogue alongside. The lacklustre range catalogue for 1966 (top left) is dated 10/65; it is a two-pager with a gatefold, and uses cut-out mono photos, with spot colour highlighting 2–4 lines of text per model. Colour returns for the BL catalogue dated 9/69 (top right), and for the final Morris range catalogue featuring the Minor (top centre), printed 9/70 for the 1971 model year. Although the last Minor saloon was produced on 12 November 1970, the catalogue, launched at the October Motor Show, depicts both saloon and Traveller.

The Morris range catalogue for the 1970 model year (dated 9/69) features the Minor alongside the 1100 Mk II saloon.

The final Minor catalogue is – at last! – a much better effort, with eight pages in upright format, stapled together. It is not, as might appear, solely for the Traveller: inside is a self-contained four pages devoted to the saloon. It is undated, but the un-retouched 'H' suffix on the registration indicates 1969–70 photography.

Three catalogues for the light commercial Minors; the blue-covered example dates from 1966, and is later shared with Austin-badged Minor vans; the red and yellow catalogue for the 'Morris ¼-ton van and pick-up Series III' is dated 12/56; the green catalogue covering both Minor and Cowley (½-ton) commercials is a 1955 issue.

This shared catalogue for the ¼-ton (Minor) and ½-ton Cowley commercials is a single sheet, unfolding to this spread. The Oxford-derived Cowley commercials are now extremely rare.

The 1956 catalogue for the 'Series III' commercials uses coloured artwork throughout, and was current for several years. Subsidiary images show Minor LCVs in foreign settings: wishful thinking, as precious few Minor commercials can have been sold to French shopkeepers, as depicted in one picture. The single 22 x 17 inch sheet folds down to the regular 11 x 8½ inch size.

Chapter Twelve

A Minor for the Millennium

WHAT IF THE Minor had continued in production? How would its styling have evolved over the three decades since 1971? This was the well-intentioned starting point for this exercise, involving four of Britain's top car stylists – Ian Callum of TWR, free-lance Peter Stevens, Peter Horbury of Volvo, and James Watkins of Rover.

The idea was for each stylist to present renderings for a Minor for the 1970s, a Minor for the '80s, and finally a Minor for the late '90s.

Obviously the exercise was going to beg various things. In particular, would the '70s car have retained rear-wheel drive? Almost certainly, as a counter-point to the front-wheel-drive 1100/1300 and because BL would probably have kept the same basic running gear, as it did for the Marina. By the '80s, however, fwd would have been a certainty, still in conjunction with the A-series engine. In the '90s it seems safe to assume use of the K-series power unit.

In the end, the notion of thinking back to how a Minor *might* have been designed in the 1970s or '80s largely defeated the team. There was simply no template for updating a late-'40s design to the '70s, let alone the '80s: the closest parallel was the quirkily French late-'60s transformation of the Citroën 2CV into the Dyane. The leap in design terms was deemed too great. Meanwhile, too, BMC had arguably offered its own 'new Minor', twice over, with first the Austin A40 then the Austin/Morris 1100. Then in the '70s there was the Marina . . .

'People are now looking back to character-formed designs, and recognising the value of them. But if you'd stood in the '70s and looked back at an old design you'd just have seen it as being old,' comments Rover styling chief Geoff Upex. 'If you'd tried to design a new Minor then, it wouldn't have looked anything like a Minor 1000. Every designer would have been trying to make it look absolutely modern – which is what happened. The Marina is really a '70s vision of what the car would have been like. In the '70s it was probably correct for the time.'

It's a question of eras, and of the more radical stylistic evolution that took place in the 1948–71 period. Evolving a VW Golf through four models while retaining a strong 'Golf' feel has proved possible, over the 1974–97 period; doing the same with a Minor, over roughly the same time-span, would have been a much greater challenge, given the stylistic and technical progress made during the Minor's life. This is a point Upex stresses:

'You cannot evolve the engineering concept without evolving the style at the same time. I really do believe there would have been a point in the '70s when the Minor would have become a completely different car, and then everybody in the '90s would have realised it was a complete mistake and would have attempted to regurgitate the Minor 1000 . . .'

And that, therefore, is where our four stylists come in: how do they envisage a Minor for the late '90s?

Peter Stevens

Peter Stevens responded to the challenge of what a new Minor might have been like during the BMC/BL era by winding the clock back to the '60s. His hypothesis is that the 'new Minor' would in fact have been an adaptation of the A40 – as launched in 1958. But is his rendering, with its extended glasshouse and add-on wood, just slightly tongue-in-cheek?

'No I don't think so. What BMC was doing at the time was to take one reasonable car and turn it into all the other models they wanted it to be. My artwork is a critique, if you like, of what BMC was doing. It could quite well have done something like this – and done it badly. At the time I was pretty appalled by what BMC was doing with cars such as the Riley Elf and

Peter Stevens

Best known as the stylist of the front-drive Lotus Elan and the McLaren F1 supercar, Peter Stevens is Britain's top freelance car designer. Trained at the Royal College of Art, he began his career at Ford, in 1970, moving to Ogle Design three years later.

In the period 1975–85 he worked as an independent, but from 1985 until 1989 he was Chief Designer, Styling, at Lotus Cars. As well as the new Elan his credits include the Excel and the restyled Esprit. After Lotus, Stevens was Chief Designer, body, interior and aerodynamics, for the JaguarSport XJR-15 supercar, before moving on to fulfil the same role at McLaren Cars, for the F1.

Since the completion of the McLaren project in 1993 he has worked as a consultant designer to Aston Martin, Lamborghini, ERF Trucks, OZ Wheels, Rolls-Royce, and many other companies.

Wolseley Hornet – they were all really tragic.'

Would BMC really have considered a 'woody' A40 with ornamental wood trim? Think back to the first Austin and Morris Mini estates: these had just such trim, specifically so that they could be mistaken at a distance for the posher

Tongue-in-cheek? Stevens says BMC might well have considered a Morris version of the Austin A40. But would it have dared go for a chopped roofline?

HERE IS YOUR NEW CAR

AUSTIN A40

AUSTIN A40

Minor Traveller with its structural wood framing.

The notion of a 'Minorised' A40 isn't outlandish, either: the square-cut Pininfarina styling gave the A40 the efficient packaging that was always an Issigonis priority. Issigonis the engineer would, however, never have countenanced the Austin's primitive mechanicals; working as he was on front-wheel drive and rubber/fluid suspensions, at the end of the '50s he would have had no truck with leaf-sprung back axles, hydro-mechanical brakes and cam-and-peg steering.

The starting point for the Stevens 'Minor for the '90s' renderings was a conversation when it was agreed that evoking the spirit of the Minor Traveller would be a fascinating challenge. The idea was for an 'honest' car, practical for both everyday and leisure use – something along the lines of Citroën's van-derived Berlingo Multispace, but with more style and originality.

The result is two renderings, of a 'Traveller' and a pick-up, both being built around the same structure. The external framing pays visual homage to the Traveller's woodwork but also echoes it in terms of function. Stevens sees the cars as being built around an exposed extruded-aluminium frame – 'an "allie" rather than a "woody", I suppose you could say . . .'

Aluminium is certainly increasingly a constructional possibility: Audi's big A8 has an aluminium spaceframe, the Lotus Elise has a bonded hull made of aluminium extrusions, and the Renault Spider has a welded aluminium hull. With such a construction, a choice of body panels could be hung around a basic hull-cum-bodyframe. These panels could be plastic, says Stevens, or they could be steel. The problem with plastic, he says, is that it takes between two and three times as long to form as a pressed-steel panel.

Turning to the styling, Stevens has avoided an over-emphasis on details inherited from the Minor. This is because he is something of a sceptic

when it comes to the current rash of 'retro' designs.

'With some other stylists I contributed some sketches to a magazine competition to restyle the Mini. Mine were non-retro, and 80 per cent of the readers voted for them. I don't think people want "retro" – I think they're just having it forced on them.'

As a consequence of such views, Stevens feels uneasy about the strongly 'retro' new Mini revealed at the 1997 Frankfurt Motor Show – something that has a definite relevance to his 'Minor for the '90s'.

'It's kind of fun and entertaining, and

With the alloy body frame, spinning off variants such as a pick-up would be straightforward.

Rover's 'Spiritual' concepts please Stevens, as a lively new way of interpreting the Mini. (Rover)

The new Mini, as revealed at the 1997 Frankfurt show, fails to convince him. It's no surprise, then, that the Stevens Minor proposals are the least 'retro' of the four presentations. (Rover)

fine as a show car. But if it's the real thing then we should be concerned. In contrast the "Spiritual" concept cars shown at the 1997 Geneva Show were just excellent. They were a really lively *new* interpretation of the Mini — and that's the way to go. If the Frankfurt Mini is representative, imagine what the same people would do if they had to come up with a new Minor . . .'

So Stevens hasn't been 'slavishly retro' with his Minor proposals — although, he says, 'the car has to have a Morris-like face'. Other than the horizontally slatted grille, the main Minor-evoking feature is the use of round headlamps pushed to the edge of the wings.

'Round lamps are infinitely cheaper. It's silly to lumber the customer for a car like this with a £120 bill for a new headlamp, when a round unit will cost £12. And once you've gone for a round headlamp, that's the obvious place to put it.

'There's another consideration. Everybody is now doing elaborately shaped Boxster-style headlamps. They'll look great for 10 minutes, then they'll start to look dated. It's a bit like the trapezoidal headlamps on a Peugeot 504. They now look very dated and cumbersome. Designers should have some sort of long-term commitment to their customers . . .'

On a lesser level, another Minor-inspired detail is the distinctive scooped door handles — a detail which all the other stylists have also incorporated in their '90s renderings.

'It's a cheap way to do a handle, and it's practical. On a car like this they don't want to be complicated. An exotically designed door handle would send the wrong message about the car. These details count: the handle is what you come up to and touch when you first approach a car.'

Finally, is there perhaps an element of the Renault Twingo about the car's stance and proportions?

'I do like the Twingo a lot, although it's slightly lacklustre from some views — from the back it looks as if the boot is full of potatoes. But it's the sort of car — along with the Ford Ka — that you pick up from an airport, as a hire car, and it makes you smile. It's a nice, friendly, jolly thing.'

Those are certainly some key aspects of the Minor's character. Stevens feels, however, that perhaps closer to what he is proposing is Renault's Kangoo van-derived estate.

'It's that sort of car — quite a lot of car for your money, and not a grotty little thing. It has to be simple, to appeal to practical-minded people — former Renault 4 and Citroën 2CV

Renault's fun-and-funky Twingo shares something of its stance and proportions with the Stevens cars, and Stevens admits to liking the bold little one-box design. (Renault)

But would something a bit bigger and more rugged, such as the Renault Kangoo, be more the type of vehicle a new Traveller should emulate? (Renault)

owners, those people who are perhaps slightly embarrassed about having to have a car . . .'

Ian Callum

As stylist of the Aston Martin DB7, a car with strong styling links to previous Astons, Ian Callum is less queasy about aesthetic references to the past.

'What's happening in car design at the moment – I feel quite positive about it and I won't call it "retro" – is that people are looking for quite strong character in their cars, as cars were perceived to have in the '50s and '60s. Everyone's rushing about trying to give their cars a face, with grilles and lamps and so on.

'I feel confident that whatever had happened to the Morris Minor, had it continued – and the next Minor was really the Marina, even if the styling went adrift somewhat – whatever had happened in the meantime, there would have been an attempt by now to revert to the characteristics people remember in the original Minor.

'So I've tried to emulate to a certain extent the cuteness – the gentleness – of the original. It's very important for any car that the overall impression as you walk towards it for the first time – something you can't really show in a

Ian Callum

Design Manager for TWR Design, 44-year-old Callum set up TWR's studios and was responsible for the design of the Aston Martin DB7. After helping shape the Volvo C70 coupé, his most recent creation is the V12 Aston Martin 'Project Vantage' concept. A graduate of the RCA, where he was sponsored by Ford, he spent 12 years at Ford in various postings around the world, culminating as manager of Ghia — where he instigated the Zig and Zag concept cars. The exterior styling of the Cosworth Escort is his work.

There are some similarities to the previous Mazda 121, which was a brave attempt to create a different sort of small car. Interestingly, the Mazda seems to appeal to non-enthusiast but style-conscious women drivers in the same way as many have taken to the Minor. (Mazda)

sketch — is that it gives off a certain aura, and I'm very sensitive to that. It's something that has nothing to do with all the obvious styling cues and is intuitive and instinctive rather than specific. If I were to work my rendering into a three-dimensional model I'd be very careful about what presence the car had, for someone seeing it for the first time.

'For my Minor I wanted to keep it simple — very simple. Cars of character, those that last a decent time, are those that have the least fuss about them. They have the strongest silhouette, the strongest stance — which I think the Minor has: put 5½Js on it and it looks terrific! — and have simple, strong but not too overt styling. That's even to the point where at a first viewing the design might appear to lack sparkle. Within a very short time such a car actually becomes seen as a very interesting vehicle.'

Callum retains the Minor's three-box configuration, with a short bustle tail evoking the Minor's curved bootline. 'A very rounded profile is important to maintain, because it's what the character of the Minor is about.'

There are perhaps shades of the previous-series Mazda 121 about the shape, a thought that doesn't over-enthuse Callum. The 121 is far too narrow, he says — and there's no reason why a Minor for the '90s should be narrow. His Minor, sized between the Fiesta and the Escort — would thus have a squat wide-track stance. It would also, unlike the Mazda, be a hatchback, for reasons of practicality — 'although I don't think that today packaging is so ultra-sensitive as it might have been a few years ago.'

Callum's design includes styled — but

not extravagantly so — headlamp units. He agrees with Peter Stevens that over-stylised headlamps could date rapidly, but is not convinced by the argument that in a high-volume car shaped lamps need cost more than round lamps.

'I wanted to get back to round head-lamps, but I didn't want just to do round lamps. I wanted to give the front some character rather than just use the cliché of a round lamp, and I still think my lamps will stand the test of time. Nowadays we have the technology to do any shape lamp we want. The reason lamps were round in the past was because that's the way everybody made them.

'Now we can do what we want, so I've attempted to bring something of a cute, honest round lamp into the design, yet do something quite individ-ual to that car so it can't be mistaken for anything else. In time what would happen is that this car would take on its own charm, because of details like that, and perhaps supersede in people's memory the original Minor.

'There's something else I was very aware of with the old Minor, and that was the low front wings of the first cars. They came off the bonnet in a lovely pure line. With my front wings I've tried to evoke something of the "lowlight" wings. I don't like the later cars with the sticking-up lamps. I wanted to keep the lines purer, and I totally sympathise with Issigonis's dis-like of the later wings. The wingline on the "lowlight" was a beautiful one and the car looked a lot chunkier for it. It seemed to have much more of a solid character — stronger and more pure — and that was something I wanted to capture. As soon as the front lamps came popping up in the air the car became a bit feminine, a bit too sweet and dainty.

'The pointed bonnet had to be there. It's such a lovely part of the car, and I thought it important to capture some of the character of that. I also thought that kick-out at the bottom of the doors was relevant. It was quite evident in the original, the way the doors flow out to what would have been the running boards.'

Another strong design element is the use of pronounced wheelarches to sug-

Ian Callum has tried to bring out the 'cuteness and gentleness' of the Minor. The pronounced wheelarches evoke the Minor's wings.

gest the Minor's wings. 'It's important to give some character to the wings. There was a tendency otherwise that they'd look a bit too modern, a bit too "today". The only way to get more exaggerated wings would have been to rebate the surfaces of the main body further into the car, and that would cut into the interior space. Hence there's a hint of the wings – just enough, without intruding too much into the volume of the packaging area.

'The profile of the roof is quite important. It's crucial, to give the car character, to have some sheet metal showing above the windscreen, so it looks like the car has a very high forehead and the screen looks more like a big porthole, as opposed to the front just being an expanse of glass.'

Where would Callum's 'new Minor' sit in the market? Would it be a mainstream model or a niche 'boutique' product such as the new Beetle or Nissan's Micra-based 'Pike series' of fun cars?

'I think to maintain its purity, or what people remember the Minor as, it would almost have to be a niche product. But you could probably take it half way between one position and the other – make it interesting enough to fall into a niche market, but cheap enough and practical enough to fall into a very real market.

'The truth is that if you want to design a modern car that is more space-efficient and cheaper to make you wouldn't end up with a reinterpreted Morris Minor. It's probably got to be square, and it's probably got to look pretty boring, like an Escort or a Golf. But I'd like to feel there's a position somewhere in the middle . . .'

James Watkins

The artwork presented by Rover stylist Watkins is more flamboyant, with the

element of exaggeration typical of 'hook' rendering — in other words one conceived to sell the basic concept rather than represent a production-ready design. But Watkins feels his main proposal, for a Minor saloon, is largely realistic.

'The main thing which would change is the stance. Designers are locked into giving their renderings huge wheels, sticking the tyres out and making the stance as attractive as possible — and I do admit that I've got a fascination with wheels, and love designing them. The wheels would probably be the biggest thing to change: you'd scale them down to something realistic, probably 16 inches rather than the 20 inches or so they are at the moment.

'Other than that, and the very thin windscreen pillars, the main thing is the lack of bumpers. You'd get around that probably with another panel that broke away from the main bonnet pressing but which from a distance would be almost invisible.'

Watkins has picked out three principal elements of the original Minor's styling: the horizontal grille bars, the waistline moulding integrating the scooped door handles, and — above all — the way the wingline is carried into the front doors.

'I've no idea how they got so much form into those doors. It's pretty astonishing, if it's a single pressing. I'm sure if you asked that of engineers today they'd scream and wave their hands in horror.

'This is the sort of project where you can take any aspect and work it up into a credible solution. You pick convenient elements which you think can be updated and you discard the rest. I like that feature line running through the door — nobody else does that. And I like the side section — it's one of the beautiful things about the Minor. I love the curves and the tension, the way the doors drift into the sill section. It's something I've picked up in the van

James Watkins

A Principal Designer on small cars at Rover Group, Watkins won a 1984 *Autocar* magazine design competition while a 15-year-old schoolboy. He went on to study at Coventry Polytechnic and, with Rover sponsorship, at the Royal College of Art. He has been at Rover since 1993 and has worked on the MGF and the facelift of the Land-Rover Discovery. Currently involved in the new Mini for 2000, his contributions to this chapter therefore have a particular relevance.

version, where I've sketched in a little step, which you could maybe use if loading things on to the roof.

'I've also evoked the horizontally slatted Minor grille, and the over-riders, which I've built into the grille. Maybe they could offer some protection, if they protruded a little more. But I think the theme of a high bonnet is no longer relevant. You couldn't justify having that size of bonnet, because there's nothing to fill it up with — not that there really was with the Minor.'

It's at this point that the question of honesty in design re-emerges: the idea, as broached by Geoff Upex, that a car's appearance should reflect its mechanical composition. Hence the compact low bonnet-line of the Watkins Minor, reflecting the imagined use of a transverse K-Series powerpack. Inevitably this raises the issue of the new Beetle, which seeks to evoke a rear-engined original while being powered by a crossways-mounted front engine.

'It's not honest,' says Watkins of the Beetle. 'When it loses so much honesty you treat it as something of an irrelevance. I didn't want to land in that trap with my Minor. The Minor was a volume-seller and if you want to repeat that it has to look fresh, contemporary, and just that little bit forward-looking, to last the distance. Otherwise it's going to be a pretty short-term thing. They didn't have post-modern irony in the days of the Minor — it was designed to sell in huge volume . . .

'What I was trying to do with the two designs was take the car in two directions, while keeping it contemporary, rather than doing a caricature "retro" design such as the new Beetle — that sort of play on the old themes but making a cartoon of it.

'I don't think Issigonis would have appreciated that. The Minor was quite contemporary — it used a lot of design themes from America, scaled down. Despite his being quoted as saying styling was a waste of time, I don't think he really felt that. He was definitely aware of the importance of correct proportions and a good stance, as the story of his widening the Minor at the last minute shows so well. If he were doing it again today he would want something that was a credible and relevant design, not something that was a bit of a joke, and a short-lasting joke at that — which I think the new Beetle will be. It's a charming thing, and you can't help but like it. But I think people will love it for a while, but then the joke will wear off, in a similar way to Nissan and its limited-edition 'Pike series' cars such as the Figaro and S-Cargo.

'I've taken as one of the themes the intersecting volumes of the car, but updated them and used sharper edges. The car has ended up a bit more aggressive than the original, which was a totally non-threatening design. But that's a consequence of today's design — it's that much more "in your face" and aggressive.'

A dominant feature of the design — which is envisaged as a hatchback — is 'clap-hands' pillarless doors, as found on various classic Lancias. 'It's a theme I've put into a lot of sketches. I think it's a very elegant detail. You can imagine that whole aperture opening up. I just love the way that in old films people get out of cars so elegantly. It's so awkward struggling around a forward-hinged door — it's much easier to

The new Beetle lacks honesty, says Watkins, who feels its appeal might be short-lived. (Volkswagen)

do it the other way. If you can put enough structure around the 'A' and 'B' posts to get away with it, I'd love to see it used. You'd need strong windscreen pillars, but you could black out the structure to make the front pillars seem slim, or else reduce their size by using ultra-high-strength steel – there's such a claustrophobic feel about so many modern thick-pillared cars that maybe there'll be a reaction against that sort of thing.'

Another unusual detail on the Watkins rendering is the one-piece bonnet-cum-front: 'I like simplifying panels, and getting two for the price of one. I could see the whole of this bonnet hinging up or else opening forward as the Herald's did. Lifting the bonnet isn't one of those everyday things any more, and if there's a bit more effort involved in opening it I don't think that matters.'

The second Watkins rendering is in strong contrast to his Minor saloon. 'Despite my previous remarks, I have done something non-aggressive for my Traveller/van. I played on the tension-less curves of the Minor and did a modernised version of the wood structure, in aluminium. The idea was a flexible system, done in an honest way, with the structure visible and real, rather than a bogus cladding. That would be very exciting: you'd be celebrating that the structure is part of the thing, rather than hiding it away.

'You could imagine the car coming in all sorts of wheelbases. It's shown as a van, with a sliding flexible cover to the sides, but you could imagine it as a Traveller, with a split around the centreline and some sort of glasshouse. It would be a nice theme to follow up and explore on Rover's computer-aided "Alias" system. I'd love to develop it further . . .

'In a way I've gone back on what I've said earlier, because I've done a slightly cartoon version, simplifying it, modernising it, choosing bits and discarding

other bits. I was keen to take the brief in two different directions, and see how it would come out.'

Peter Horbury

Volvo Design Director Horbury was brave enough to tackle a 1970s Minor, producing a rendering with a surprisingly modern feel. 'It's very difficult to project one's thoughts back to the '70s without automatically doing the nostalgia bit we'd do today,' he says. 'Back in the '70s we'd almost certainly have done a square car.'

The key element of the Horbury '70s presentation is a waistline with something of the current Bentley Continental about it – but then the Bentley itself evokes the '60s Coke-bottle shape of the two-door Rolls-Royce Silver Shadow and Corniche.

Nissan's humorous little Figaro (top) was another ephemeral 'retro' design, reckons Watkins – as was its fellow 'Pike series' car, the Pao runabout. (Nissan)

Peter Horbury was brave enough to tackle a Minor for the '70s: he sought inspiration from the controversial 'Coke-bottle' Cortina Mk III.

'I looked for inspiration in the Cortina of the time. Because the Minor has such a strong shape, and such a lot of form, with its separate wingline, I took the strongly formed Coke-bottle line from the Escort and Cortina Mk III and developed that in a Minoresque way. I used Minor cues, but translated the Minor's separate wingline into Ford's Coke-bottle.'

Another Minor motif is the high bonnet line, both as a styling device and as a reflection, says Horbury, of the old-fashioned Marina mechanicals that would undoubtedly have been hiding underneath. Other features evoking the original are the horizontal-slat grille, and the outboard slightly protruding position of the headlamps.

'My car gives an idea of how the Minor might have developed, while remaining a Morris Minor. It's the sort of thing which might have happened if instead of doing the square-ish Marina some product planner in the company had been frightened enough not to destroy the Minor, even though the '70s way of thinking was all-change. Maybe because the Cortina was such a popular car it would have been a guide.

'It's complete with the very rounded Minor roof, something which caused some debate at Volvo, over whether it was appropriate. It also has huge plastic bumper end-caps, plus over-riders. I don't think we understood enough about integrated bumpers then – we were just starting to experiment. So I kept to separate bumpers.

'The '90s car is more reminiscent of the Minor. I think that's probably more appropriate in the '90s, because there's a lot more form in designs today. The late '70s and the '80s destroyed the

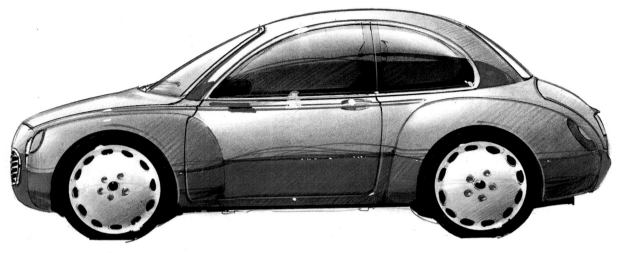

three-dimensional sculpted form of cars — the square-cut Giugiaro look was prevalent, and the Sierra was on its own for a while as a car with rounded forms. It was one of the first — after the Porsche 928. The design language of the '90s is resurrecting a lot more of this three-dimensional form.'

There's also the trend for 'retro' design influencing the return to more curvaceous forms, and here Horbury is keen to tread carefully.

'In the '90s we have no problems about bringing back styling cues from the past. But I didn't want to make a copy of the Minor. I think the new Beetle, even though it's very nicely done, is such a copy. That's where the danger of the new Mini comes to mind. If the car is meant to be a serious car in any way, it shouldn't just blatantly copy the original.

'One of the Minor cues I picked out was the separate wingline — it's very much alive and kicking today. Another thing that is very good about the Minor, and which lends itself to a modern car, is the round roof. I think that translates very well into the '90s.

'The car benefits from modern tech-

nology and so has soft-nose bumpers that don't protrude. The headlamps are round — maybe they should have been square in my '70s proposal — and are back where they should be. I was thinking back to the "lowlight" Minor and to the sort of thing that would make a difference to a modern car, and add a bit of quirkiness — some sort of recognition point. With modern technology you're more free to move things around.'

Although Horbury shares his colleagues' admiration of the Renault Twingo, he feels that if any 'modern' has influenced his thoughts on a Minor for the '90s it has been Nissan's current Micra.

'If lately any car has been a replacement for the Minor it is the Nissan Micra. It's certainly caught some of the customers for the Minor. So you'll see some resemblance to the Micra in my '90s rendering, although with its separate wingline it's a lot more three-dimensional. It's interesting that the Japanese are very keen on making a car look happy. Like the Micra, then, my Minor is a friendly, cheeky car, a bit of fun, and not too serious — and I think that's what appeals to the Minor owner.'

For the '90s proposal Horbury had no qualms about introducing a more 'retro' feel – and is there a touch of the second-generation Richard Oakes Midas about those 'suggested' wings?

Chapter Thirteen

Which
Minor is which?

'Lowlight' Series MM

Years current: 1948–51
Body styles: Two-door saloon, two-door Tourer
Number made: Total all MMs 176,002 (estimated 'lowlight' approx 63,000)

This is the Minor with the shape as Alec Issigonis intended, with small 5-inch headlamps low-set within the front panel. Power comes from the side-valve 918cc engine used in the preceding Morris Eight Series E. The four-speed gearbox also comes from the Eight, and has a long non-remote floor lever.

With the exception of a few very late transitional cars, all 'lowlights' have two-piece bumpers back and front. This is a legacy of when Issigonis decided at the last moment to widen the Minor by 4 inches, after bumper tooling had already been ordered.

Key production changes to the 'lowlight' are the fitting of a second round rear light in March 1949, followed by a move to triangular 'helmet' rear light units in June 1949, and the availability from October 1950 of a water pump and a heater as optional equipment. Until November 1950, home-market cars also had to make do with only a single wiper.

The last 'lowlight' cars were produced in January 1951. Most were exported, but sufficient were made for

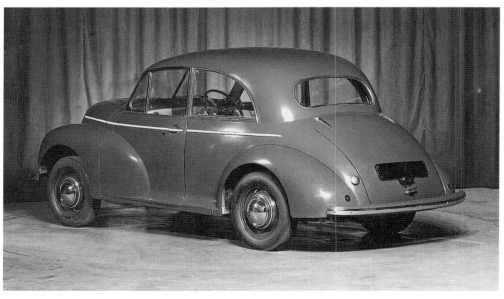

This launch photo of the Minor shows what is probably a pre-production car – note the single-piece rear bumper and the fully painted waistline moulding. The 'frenched' rear light and reflector disappeared within a few months. (Nuffield/Haymarket)

a reasonable number to have survived in Britain. Expect slow but still usable performance and a rather pre-war gearchange; in compensation the taut handling and precise steering are well ahead of what the opposition was offering at the time.

'Highlight' Series MM

Years made: 1950–53
Body styles: Two-door saloon, four-door saloon, Tourer/Convertible
Number made: Total all MMs 176,002 (estimated 'highlight' approx 113,000)

Although Minors exported to the United States had 'highlight' wings from the start of US sales in 1949, the revised wingline was only introduced to the UK with the October 1950 announcement of the four-door saloon – and this new model, always with single-piece bumpers, was initially billed as 'export only'. In January 1951 the two-door and the Tourer received the new front, which from March 1951 had a painted rather than a chromed grille. All British-market 'highlight' MMs should have one-piece bumpers, whereas two-door US cars made up to

January 1951 should in theory all have split bumpers.

In June 1951 the Tourer was given integral glass rear side-windows in place of lift-off celluloid sidescreens, and was renamed the Convertible. From August 1951 a new design of bonnet was fitted to the MM. Longer than the original type, it extends further into the scuttle and right back to the door aperture – whereas the 'short' bonnet results in a section of scuttle bridging the gap between bonnet and door.

With the arrival of the one-piece

The Tourer tested by The Motor in 1950 is here shown with its sidescreens removed. This was the last year of the 'lowlight'. (Haymarket)

The MM four-door saloon: an interesting picture, as it shows how on the four-door the plain hubcaps of the MM are matched to wheels without the painted line found on 'lowlight' wheels. The bonnet is of the 'short' type. (Haymarket)

watch you'd probably also discover that the less aerodynamically efficient front has shaved just a sliver off the car's performance.

'Cheesegrater grille' Series II

Years made: 1952–54
Body styles: two-door saloon, four-door saloon, Convertible, Traveller
Number made: Total all Series II 269,838

A later MM Convertible lifts a wheel in a '50s Cambridge University Automobile Club speed trial. (Haymarket)

This 'cheesegrater grille' Series II Convertible displays the 'long' bonnet. You can tell it's a SII by the bonnet-top mascot and the bonnet badge with the long tail. (BMC/Haymarket)

bumpers, with their curved blades, over-riders front and rear became an option. On the subject of brightwork, for March–September 1951 hubcaps were painted rather than chromed, owing to the nickel shortage provoked by the Korean War.

The last four-door MM was produced in January 1953, with the two-door and Convertible being discontinued the following month.

The 'highlight' MMs drive no differently from the mechanically identical 'lowlight' cars, although the extra weight of the four-door inevitably blunts speed somewhat. Against a stop-

Physically identical to a 'highlight' MM, the first type of Series II uses the original 803cc version of the A-series engine, with the matching Austin four-speed gearbox. The only way you can distinguish a late MM from a '52–'54 Series II is by the latter's use of a bonnet-top mascot and a bonnet badge with a long tail; however, some export cars retain the MM's smaller badge and bonnet-top chrome strip.

The SII was announced in July 1952 as an export-only four-door, and was sold alongside the side-valve MM four-door and the other MMs until these were discontinued at the beginning of 1953. In October 1953 the Traveller joined the range, and at the same time a De Luxe specification was introduced for all models. This featured leather

upholstery, a heater (on home-market cars), a passenger's sun-visor, and bumper over-riders; on the De Luxe Traveller there was in addition carpeted front wheelarches (the floor having rubber matting) and a load-floor covering with rubbing strips.

The Traveller brought in the use of an Austin three-quarters-floating back axle in place of the old-fashioned but more robust Morris semi-floating unit; in January 1954 this axle was standardised across the range.

The Series II seems at first drive surprisingly zippy, given the small size of the 30bhp Austin engine. But it soon becomes apparent that this is because the overall gearing is very low, thanks to the lower back axle ratio brought in with the new engine and gearbox. At suburban speeds this may be fine, but on the open road the engine is turning too fast. The ratios of the Austin gearbox are also very widely spaced. As a result you can be in top, with performance tailing away, and find yourself fighting the poor synchromesh and woolly knitting-needle gearlever to

bridge the gap between top and third gears.

The poor engine and gearbox are also not noted for their robustness, so many SIIs have been re-equipped with 948cc or 1098cc engines and gearboxes. Generally these are used with the short remote-control gearchange of these later cars, but the spindly SII direct-acting gearlever can be retained if one wishes.

If you like the style of an early SII, it is certainly a satisfactory solution to fit a later engine, gearbox and back axle; you might also consider uprating the brakes to 1098cc specification.

'Slatted grille' Series II

Years made: 1954–56
Body styles: as 'Cheesegrater grille' SII
Number made: Total all Series II 269,838

This is a modernised Series II, forming a stylistic bridge between the MM and Minor 1000. It retains the split wind-

The 'facelifted' Series II still has a split screen, but there is a new slatted grille; today SII Travellers such as this are very rare. (BMC/Haymarket)

enough, remains as before, while inside, with the unadorned open-glovebox dashboard, there is a little less style about the appointments. The old-fashioned mottled wire-spoke steering-wheel remains, however, as does a design of handbrake that dates back to the '30s.

Minor 1000 (948cc)

Years made: 1956–62
Body styles: as before
Number made: 544,048

The Minor 1000 is a major leap forward in Minor evolution. Gone is the weak and feebly performing 803cc engine and its 'magic wand' gearchange, and gone is the archaic split windscreen and old-fashionedly small rear window.

The new engine is of 948cc, and is considerably more robust, with a stronger crankshaft, more modern bearing material, and beefed-up conrods. The gearbox has better synchromesh and closer ratios, and there is a short remote change. With a more useful 37bhp, thankfully a higher-ratio back axle is fitted.

screen and (in saloon form) the small rear window of preceding Minors, but incorporates a new slatted grille that is carried through to the Minor 1000. It also has a new and plainer dashboard with a single central dial, and this also is continued on the Minor 1000.

Other than these two fundamental changes, the 'facelift' SII is pretty much the same as the 1952–54 cars, the only other difference of note being a new pattern of upholstery with a vertical rather than horizontal motif.

Evolutionary changes to slatted-grille SIIs are few. The most visible is a move to a new style of rounded rear light units on cars made after late 1954.

The driving experience, naturally

Larger screens front and rear identify the Minor 1000. These two saloons were caught on camera doing battle at a 1958 race meeting. Visible under both cars is a front anti-roll bar. (Tom March/Autosport)

Externally, the Minor is transformed by the large curved front screen, bringing with it more slender pillars, and by the generous wraparound rear window – mirrored on the Convertible by the fitting of a larger celluloid panel to the hood. A final touch is deeper rear wings on the saloons and the Convertible, and the observant will also notice slightly different rear lights, with a large chrome base replacing the painted plinth and chrome bezel of 'facelift' Series II Minors.

Inside, the gloveboxes now both have lids, there's a new dished three-branch steering wheel, and a more modern push-button handbrake. Upholstery on early 1000s is as on the preceding SIIs, but a squarer design of seat was soon introduced.

In March 1957 the fuel tank was increased from a niggardly 5-gallon capacity to a more appropriate $6^1/_2$ gallons, and in September that year the Convertible's hood material changed from canvas to plastic.

In 1959 the gloveboxes gained bright finishers, giving a further lift to the dashboard, and at the same time the upholstery changed to a pattern of broader flutes with a horizontal panel across the top.

Other changes to the 948cc Minor 1000 were few. During the period August–November 1961 first the trafficators were at last replaced by flashers, then the De Luxe versions received duo-tone upholstery, and finally, in November, the gloveboxes lost their lids again. As a consequence of the move to duo-tone upholstery, leather was no longer part of the De Luxe specification.

The 948cc Minor 1000 is an infinitely better car to drive than a Series II. It has zippy performance, a slick gearchange, and is well up to holding its own in modern traffic. With the steering wheel still having charming wire spokes and with the golden-faced speedo, the push-pull switches and the

separate starter knob, there's still plenty that's quaint about the 948cc cars, yet they have made a quantum jump in usability.

Minor 1000 (1098cc)

Years made: 1962–71
Body styles: as before
Number made: 303,443

The early 1098cc Minors are a car further improved, yet still with all the charm of the preceding Minor 1000s. Internally and externally, the first year of 1098cc Minors, made from September 1962 until October 1963, are identical to the 948cc cars: the only difference is under the bonnet.

Here there is a considerably improved power unit, with a strengthened crankcase, a stronger crankshaft, and an output of 48bhp; this drives

Glovebox lids arrived with the Minor 1000. Clearly visible in this launch-time BMC photo is the new remote change for the gearbox. The patterned trim was not used on production 1000s – this car, with its well-worn gearlever paint and good number of miles on the clock, is clearly a pre-production development hack. (BMC/Haymarket)

A very late 1098cc Traveller displays the post-'63 twin rear lights. Carrying capacity in the Traveller is impressive. (James Mann/Classic & Sports Car)

A 1965 Convertible shows the bigger front lamp units introduced in October 1963 and the heat-formed trim brought in for the 1965 model year. (Haymarket)

through a bigger clutch to a beefed-up gearbox with improved (baulk-ring) synchromesh, then to a higher-ratio back axle. At the same time the front brakes are better, thanks to wider drums and a smaller bore for the master cylinder and the rear wheel cylinders.

In October 1963 the Minor was modernised by the introduction of bigger front and rear lamp units incorporating separate flashers. This was a vast improvement on the cheese-paring old arrangement whereby a relay cut out the appropriate sidelight or stop light when one wanted to indicate. At the same time the 'clap-hands' wipers were replaced by an orthodox tandem mechanism and the passenger's door gained a key lock.

The last round of changes came in October 1964, when the interior was restyled. The revised dashboard incorporates a black-faced central dial set in a patterned aluminium panel, and has a lid for the passenger's glovebox. A new two-spoke plastic steering wheel and a combined key-operated ignition and starter further update the controls, while the upholstery and trim is in a single-tone heat-formed vinyl. At the same time as these changes, the tip-and-fold front passenger seat on two-door models disappeared in favour of a simple tipping seat.

It was in this format that the Minor ended its days, neglected by an ailing BMC, then left unexploited by an incompetent BL with other priorities. In June 1969 the Convertible was discontinued, in November 1970 the saloons, and finally in April 1971 the last Traveller left the lines.

The 1098cc Minor 1000s are the most common, and offer improved performance and better braking. The bigger engine does make a difference, and nobody should have any qualms about using the car as everyday transport. The post-'64 interior is less agreeable, but still well-presented in the no-nonsense functional style so typical of all Minors.

Series II commercials

Years made: 1953–56
Body styles: Van and pick-up
Number made: 48,513

There are no MM commercials, and it was May 1953 before the Series II LCVs (light commercial vehicles) were announced. Power comes from a low-compression version of the 803cc ohv engine, with a high-compression engine available as an option.

The commercial Minors are built on a separate chassis, and this brings with it the use of telescopic rear dampers. The bonnet is plain, with no mouldings

and with the MM style of badge and chrome strip. A shorter painted bumper blade is used at the front, and at the rear there are merely two rubber buffers.

Neither flashers nor trafficators are standard equipment, although later GPO vans have roof-top 'elephant's ear' flashers. The very earliest LCVs have fixed front quarter-lights, and all Series II variants have a plain rubber screen surround with no bright insert, plus a central screen pillar painted body colour rather than chromed. Inside, trim is kept to the minimum, and cars built up until February 1955 have a simple wooden dashboard. After that date the 'facelift' grille and accompanying dash are used.

Series II commercials are particularly rare, most having been driven into the ground during a hard working life. If you find a restorable example, don't hesitate: go for it!

Series III & Series V commercials

Years made: 1956–72
Body styles: Van and pick-up
Number made: 100,613 Series III and 177,483 Series V

Manufactured from September 1956,

the Series III commercials use a low-compression version of the 948cc engine (with a high-compression option) and have the remote gearchange of the passenger cars. The body, naturally enough, has the one-piece screen of the Minor 1000.

The Series V (the tag Series IV was used for the Mini LCVs) is the commercial counterpart to the 1098cc Minor, and was introduced in September 1962. The switch to the

This early SII van has been converted to estate format by Cowley. The bonnet with no moulding is clearly visible, as is the shorter painted front bumper blade. (BMC/author's collection)

Post Office vans

The Post Office was the major fleet user of Minor vans, taking 52,745 in all, and a good many surviving LCVs are ex-GPO. All 'cheesegrater-grille' Post Office vans (as made until early 1955) had the unusual feature of rubber front wings, with separate headlamps perched on top; the idea was to cut down on minor body repairs. In addition, all but the last split-screen GPO vans had an opening screen on the driver's side.

Amused and confused? There's more: the GPO continued to be supplied with split-screen vans until 1959, and even after going over to the Minor 1000 cab the poor posties and Post Office engineers had to tolerate the 803cc engine and its 'knitting-needle' gearchange right through to 1964. In August of that year GPO vans received the 1098cc engine and matching gearbox, followed in January 1965 by the final-style dashboard introduced at the same time on the 'civvy' LCVs. That means that there were no GPO vans with the 948cc engine and its accompanying gearbox.

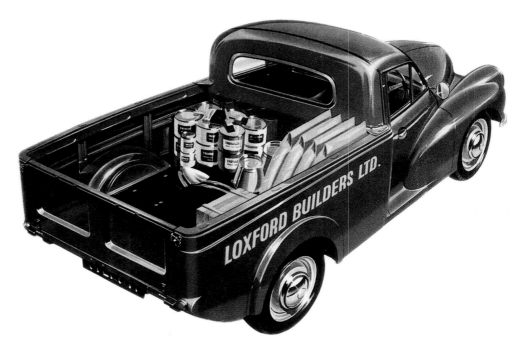

Typical BMC brochure artwork admirably depicts the loadspace area of the Minor 1000 pick-up. (Author's collection)

1098cc engine and its matching gearbox brings with it an increase in maximum payload to 6cwt, along with the recog-

---

'I never knew that . . .'

- Early four-door MMs – until August/September 1951 – have a chrome surround to the rear screen.
- All 'highlight' saloons have a moulding running around the rear body between the roof turret and the rear deck.
- Before the arrival of the Minor 1000, there were no badges fitted to the rear doors of the Traveller.
- Series II Travellers, whether standard or De Luxe, never had carpet in the passenger compartment.
- The 'Disabled Person's Car' was a Minor 1000 blessed with the old 803cc Series II engine and its matching gearbox. Carrying the SII's bonnet badging and boot badge, it was only available as a two-door. Latterly a 1098cc version replaced this odd hybrid: it was just like an ordinary Minor apart from the use of plain door and side trim panels and the fitment of special easy-action sliding seat runners.
- All Minor saloons have a rear seat with a folding back.
- Some of the last Travellers and commercials have a steering-column lock. This feature is also found on some earlier export models.
- Contrary to what you may have read in certain national newspapers, the Morris Minor is not still in production, in Sri Lanka or anywhere else.

---

nition point of enlarged rear windows on the van.

The new lighting arrangements for the 1964 model year arrived at about the same time as for the passenger cars, and the restyled dashboard was incorporated in January 1965 – only without a passenger-side glovebox lid.

In April 1968 the maximum payload was increased to 8cwt, thanks to stronger front uprights, beefier rear springs, and a move to $4^1/_2$J wheels; at the same time an Austin version was introduced, complete with a crinkly Austin-style grille.

Production of Minor LCVs ended in February 1972, nearly a year after the last Traveller had left the lines.

Fair numbers of Minor 1000 LCVs survive, helped by the considerable quantity of vans used by the GPO. Pick-ups are more scarce than vans, but pick-up fanciers need not despair: Minor panels specialist Henric offers reproduction pick-up backs in glass-fibre (as well as grp van rear bodies), so you can always build up your own pick-up using a van as a basis for the conversion.

Index

Endpaper illustrations: Two charming images
from the original Series MM Owner's Handbook.